EXTRUDED
CERAMICS

EXTRUDED CERAMICS

TECHNIQUES ■
PROJECTS ■
INSPIRATIONS ■

DIANA PANCIOLI

LARK BOOKS
A Division of Sterling Publishing., Inc.
New York

EDITOR: **Danielle Truscott**
ART DIRECTOR: **Kathleen Holmes**
ASSISTANT EDITOR: **Catharine Sutherland**
PRODUCTION ASSISTANT: **Hannes Charen**

Library of Congress Cataloging-in-Publication Data
Pancioli, Diana.
    Extruded ceramics : techniques, projects, inspirations /
Diana Pancioli. —1st ed.
      p.   cm.
    ISBN 1-57990-130-1
    1. Pottery craft.   2. Extrusion process.   I. Title.
TT920.P35 1999
738.1'42—dc21   99-27802
                            CIP

10 9 8 7 6 5 4 3 2 1

First Edition

Published by Lark Books, a division of
Sterling Publishing Company, Inc.
387 Park Avenue South, New York, N.Y. 10016

Distributed in Canada by Sterling Publishing,
c/o Canadian Manda Group, One Atlantic Ave., Suite 105l
Toronto, Ontario, Canada M6K 3E7

Distributed in Australia by Capricorn Link (Australia) Pty Ltd., P.O.
Box 6651, Baulkham Hills, Business Centre NSW 2153, Australia

If you have questions or comments about this book, please contact:
Lark Books
50 College St.
Asheville, NC 28801
(828) 253-0467

Printed in China by Donnelley Bright Sun Printing Company Ltd.

ISBN 1-57990-130-1

Cover:
RANDY JOHNSTON, see page 79

Back Cover top to bottom:
FRANK BOSCO, see page 43
D. HAYNE BAYLESS, see page 64

Title page:
PHILLIP SELLERS, see page 81

Following page from top to bottom:
DIANA PANCIOLI, see page 54
MICHAEL SHERRILL, see page 16
KATHY ORNISH, see page 131
PHYLLIS KUDDER-SULLIVAN, see page 84

CONTENTS

FOREWORD

While the use of clay extrusion by potters is relatively recent, clay extrusion is not quite as young—nor as limited—as might generally be believed. As early as the beginning of the 19th century, many of the pipes made to carry water and sewage were made of clay extruded with hand-operated machines and fired to stoneware temperatures. In the United States today, the manufacture of clay sewer, flue, and roofing tile is accomplished with large hydraulic extruders. Throughout the world, modern electronics and space age industries require sophisticated forms using very specialized clay bodies.

The principle of extrusion is the same whether used to produce highly technical tiles as components for astral travel or solar energy, the tiles that keep the rain off our heads, or the creative work of the studio potter. Studio potters began to use extrusion when hand-operated extruders first appeared on the market in the early 1970s. At Scott Creek, designing the first studio extruder was the result of many frustrating weekends of pulling handles for cups, mugs, and casseroles my apprentices and helpers had made during the previous week. It started with the need to extrude a solid coil as a handle for a pot, to be used when making multiple pots. Accomplishing this saved much time and work, and it was easy, then, to design casserole and teapot handles with my own distinctive look.

Today, potters use the extruder as a design aid and an adjunct to other tools in the studio. The extruded form—whether a hollow tube, a ribbon, or a flat tile—is inherently stable and makes an excellent component for joining with more traditionally made thrown and slab pieces. Possibilities for its use have expanded and continue to expand, and with them a wide range of models of extruders in different shapes, sizes, and materials.

As potters, we need not be limited by the format of the simple extruded shape. All artists working beyond the simple production of handles and coils have begun to develop beautiful forms by designing clay works specifically for creation by the extruder. This tool, perhaps more than any other at our fingertips, can become a strong force for new approaches to the forming of clay objects.

This book will be a tremendous asset to any studio potter, either beginner or professional. Good luck, and happy experimenting.

Al Johnsen
Scott Creek Pottery

RANDY JOHNSTON,
Triple Stacking Box, 1999. 9 x 5 x 11 inches (22.5 x 12.5 x 27.5 cm). Stoneware with fluxed kaolin slip; extruded, altered, and assembled; wood-fired to cone 10.
Photo by Peter Lee.

INTRODUCTION

Until now, everyone who has worked with an extruder has learned by trial and error. With this book, I hope that those readers who are not yet or are partially acquainted with extrusion will learn faster and more easily, bypassing the more common and avoidable pitfalls of the extrusion process. As potters who are familiar with extrusion know, the potential for using extrusion in pottery is boundless and still mostly unexplored. The works by clay artists featured in this book show some of the best art made to date with extrusion. My wish is that this book will inspire enthusiasm for the tool, and prompt new directions for its use.

The book's organization is straightforward. Chapters 1 through 3 offer information on basic things you need to know to begin working with extrusion—extruders (both manufactured and homemade) and some basic clay-working tools, dies and how to make them, and clay body formulation for extrusion. Chapter 4 and 5 deal with extrusion techniques using relatively simple dies—respectively, using extrusion as support while handbuilding, and using extrusion for mold making. Chapter 4 offers a good beginner's project; chapter 5 is geared toward production, in that it shows how to use extrusion to make models and produce molds to make multiples of a clay work or object.

The next few chapters, 6 through 9, provide information on a range of different techniques for using extrusion, presented relative to the complexity of dies required for each—from dies for simple, solid extrusions, to those used to create two- and three-sided forms, and finally to more complicated hollow round and square shapes. Each chapter includes a step-by-step project to guide beginners through different techniques and processes, and to illustrate possibilities for all readers. The last two chapters present more specialized subjects—using extrusion for making tiles and sculpture.

Most of the eight projects in chapters 2 and 4 through 10 are unfinished—no particular glaze treatment or firing temperature is suggested. They are intended as stimulus for further investigation into extrusion's possibilities, rather than as ends in themselves. I have also included a number of die designs which I find useful. They are primarily for use with a 4-inch-barrel extruder (a 3¼-inch die area), although a few dies for use with a 5-inch-barrel extruder are included, too. The die drawings can be photocopied, traced, and enlarged to suit your needs. You can use them as you find them, or as a starting point from which to begin designing your own dies, altering them to satisfy requirements particular to the kind of work you choose to make, and your own aesthetic sensibilities.

I bought a simple, hand-cranked extruder when the first models invented for potters came out in the early 1970s; the content of this book reflects many of my own experiments with a 4-inch-barrel extruder. Even after 20 years, I continue to like its simplicity, although I recently purchased a larger extruder for the studio at Eastern Michigan University where I teach, and have been excited by the new and expanded possibilities it offers. Many individuals and schools include standard manual extruders among their potters' equipment, and my intention in writing this book is to assist them in expanding their repertoires of uses for extruders they already own. Basically, the principles both for using a manual extruder and for making dies translate from one extruder to another, regardless of its manufacturer, shape, or size. (Even with power extrusion, the same principles apply, with the exceptions that dies must be made of sturdier materials, and considerations regarding clay flow in the extrusion process present a more complex set of problems.)

When I first used my extruder, I made a few simple plastic dies myself and had a local machinist make a few hollow dies for me. I used the tool off and on for the next decade, but didn't fully explore its uses and possibilities until graduate school in the 1980s. I spent the first year of graduate school extruding madly, making mostly sculptural work. In my second year, I incorporated extrusion into utilitarian works, and in the ensuing years have used it regularly for various purposes.

I try to bring a wheel-thrown aesthetic to the functional work I make with extrusion; I often mix methods—throwing, pressing, extruding—and enjoy when parts made by different processes work together as a whole. Mixing extrusion with other forming methods makes the work more interesting, and I enjoy the fact that it is sometimes difficult to discern which part was made by which method.

Others who extrude have told me they prefer that extrusion look exactly like what it is, rather than in more worked or manipulated forms that appear other than extruded. Potters who use extrusion seem to find themselves in particular camps: those who use it to create utilitarian ware, those who use it to make sculpture, those who use extruded forms for their mechanical nature, and those who alter the forms' inherent mechanical qualities. It's good to understand that all these directions are possible, and worth exploring—from them, we can discover our own inclinations toward extrusion. Happy extruding!

CHAPTER ONE

EXTRUDERS AND BASIC CLAYWORKING TOOLS

JOHN GLICK, *Wall Relief "Mantel Series" Diptych, 1998.* 11 x 31 x 6 inches (27.5 x 77.5 x 15 cm). Stoneware; extruded, altered (mantel portion), and wheel thrown, with press molded additions; soda fired to cone 10. Photo by artist.

ONE OF THE BEST things about creating extruded clay works is that you don't need much to get started—an extruder, some dies and clay, a few basic tools, and a little elbow grease will do the trick.

Because using dies—and especially creating your own dies—is essential to producing varied and interesting extruded forms, chapter 2 provides information on both ready-made dies and how to design and make your own. Chapter 3 offers information on the best types of clay to use for extrusion, other aspects of the process, and tips on how to anticipate and solve problems you may encounter when extruding.

In this chapter, you'll become familiar with extruders, how they work, and how to use them. The following pages also list some clay-working tools that you will need when working with extruded forms. Most potters' studios will already include these common hand tools. As you experiment with extrusion, you may discover that additional hand tools and/or motorized tools will best serve your working process. But if you are just getting started working with an extruder, you won't need more than this handful of items to create the projects presented in this book. Once you understand the techniques, you can use them to make any kind of work you want, whether functional or sculptural, small or large, simple or complex.

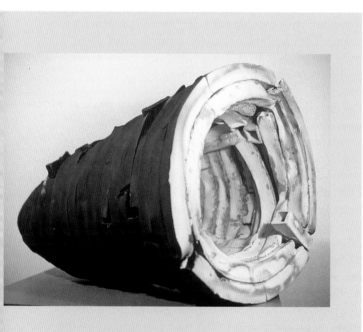

KATHY DAMBACH, *Black Hole*, 1990. 44 x 33 x 33 inches (110 x 82.5 x 82.5 cm). Stoneware; extruded and altered.

EXTRUDERS

An extruder is a simple machine, made of few parts, easy to use, and easy to care for. Simply put, an extruder is a barrel fitted with a hinged plunger and a die holder which keeps a die firmly in place at one end. Clay placed in the extruder is forced through the barrel and die, producing a seamless clay form in a hollow or solid shape determined by the shape of the die.

Extruders come in a range of sizes, shapes, and materials, and can be powered manually, electrically, or by pneumatic (air pressure) or hydraulic (water pressure) systems. Likewise, their mechanical components operate with some variation from model to model. As with all machines whose models vary in power and size, different extruders work better for different things. This book focuses on the most common studio extruder, a manual model with a 4- or 5-inch-diameter (10 or 12.5 cm) barrel. But you may discover that a small, hand-held extruder that operates like a garlic press or caulking gun is all you need to create decorative or useful objects. At the other end of the spectrum, some experience and experimentation may make it clear that a large, powerful, motorized extruder best satisfies the extrusion demands for the works you choose to make. Or you may opt, as some artists do, to design and build your own.

MANUAL EXTRUDERS

STANDARD MANUAL STUDIO EXTRUDERS

Affordable and widely available, these hand-cranked extruders are multi-purpose workhorses in the studio. They can be used with a wide range of ready-made and homemade dies and perform the simplest tasks well, such as making coils, bands, and tubes. But their capabilities are diverse: Along with coils, they can extrude other small items such as spouts and handles; medium-sized items such as boxes, lids, and trays; and components for murals, installations, and other large-scale architectural works. Their versatility, simplicity, and relative economy make them a good long-term bet for both professional and recreational potters.

Standard manual studio extruders, such as the one used in this book to demonstrate techniques, have round or square barrels of 4-, 5-, or 6-inch (10, 12.5, or 15 cm) "diameters"; the barrel is often mounted on a back bar. (There are some variations: One manufacturer offers a 3-inch [7.5 cm] barrel, and a few extruders have rectangular barrels.) The diameter of the barrel determines the size of extrusions that can be produced, although some models can be fitted with or are built including a 9-inch (22.5 cm) expansion box, an attachment for creating larger extrusions (see page 30). Extruders with square and round barrels are similarly efficient, although square-barreled extruders offer an advantage—a square barrel produces extrusions slightly larger than a round barrel of the same dimensions. A 4-inch (10 cm) round-barreled extruder can extrude forms slightly less than 4 inches (10 cm) in diameter. Because you can design dies on the diagonal for a square-barreled extruder, a 4-inch (10 cm) square-barreled extruder can make extrusions up to approximately 5½ inches (13.8 cm). The tops of some square-barreled extruders are also angled to facilitate loading clay. *(Note: A 4-inch [10 cm] extruder barrel that is about 12 inches [30 cm] long will take 10 or 11 pounds [4.54 or 4.99 kg] of clay; a 5-inch [12.5 cm] barrel of the same length will take approximately 15 pounds [6.81 kg].)*

For maximum versatility, some manufacturers offer extruders with a system of differently sized barrels that can be fitted to a single frame.

Although extruder barrels can be made of aluminum, plastic, or stainless steel, most are made of painted steel. Extruders with painted steel barrels are less expensive. They are better used with buff and darker colored clay bodies (such as stonewares and terra-cottas) that won't be harmed by the occasional iron spot released from the barrel's metal. Porcelains, or other white bodies which need to be free of any iron stains, are better used with aluminum, plastic, or stainless steel barrels.

Clay is loaded into the top of the barrel, and pushed through it by a plunger attached at a pivot point to a handle or lever. The handle is cranked down to force the clay through the barrel. Leverage required to push clay through the barrel depends on the size of the barrel (actually the square measure of the plunger face), the opening of the die, and the length of the handle. Wider barrels and smaller die openings require more force and a longer lever. As a rule, extruders come with a standard handle length that can be extended with a simple piece of pipe when greater leverage is required. (One manufacturer provides a second, longer handle.) Although it doesn't take great strength to operate a manual extruder, your own upper body fitness plays a part in the process and may actually improve after some mild workouts with it. (It's a great way to exercise and pursue art at the same time!)

On different models of manual extruders, the handle operates in tandem with the plunger in different ways. With the simplest type, force from cranking the handle causes a plunger to push clay evenly and continuously through the barrel; the plunger is long enough, relative to the barrel's length, to empty the barrel using a single, fixed pivot point. On others with shorter plungers, force exerted by handle and plunger is mediated by a notched back bar that allows the plunger to ratchet down the barrel in stages. A variation on this type has a U-bolt around a plain pipe back bar that achieves the same end as the notches: The U-bolt stays in place on the downward crank, dropping to the next position when the handle is lifted. The U-bolt alternately drops and catches, ratcheting down the back bar a small distance at a time.

Clay pushed through the barrel is forced through a die held in position by an external die holder at the

extruder's other end. Die holders vary, depending on the type of extruder you are using. Some are hung from two protruding pins sticking out on either side of the barrel which fit into grooves on the die holder. Some are held with multiple pins, two on opposite sides of a square barrel, or equidistant around a circular barrel. The loose pins are pushed through holes in the die holder into holes in the barrel. Another type of die holder has threaded bolts on each side which fit through holes in the die holder and matching holes in the barrel; they are tightened with a specialty wrench. Still another has threaded bolts and wing nuts which tighten to keep the die holder in place.

A disadvantage of a holder that is hung rather than pinned is that although it can be quickly attached, it may not always hang perfectly perpendicular to the barrel. The die holders with plain and threaded pins take longer to attach (and the pins can get lost), but the die holder is always perpendicular to the barrel.

PARTS, ATTACHMENTS, AND VARIATIONS

INTERNAL DIE HOLDERS

Some dies for hollow extrusion require that a manual extruder be fitted with an internal die holder, an extra device to hold the die's center profile in place. Manufactured internal die holders are made of metal and vary in design. One looks like a three-legged spider; another is shaped like an H. The center of the "spider" holder has a post which threads into a hole to hold the center part of the die; the three legs attach to the edge of the outer section of the die. The spider mechanism sits an inch (2.5 cm) or so above the die face in the barrel and allows the clay to move around its legs and heal (rejoin) before it exits as a hollow form. The H-holder has a center

11

post at its cross bar and its legs rest on the inside rim of the external die holder. Another manufacturer has designed an internal die holder with a Z-shaped piece that fits across both parts of the top of the die face. The Z-brace sits very close to the face of the die and allows less room for healing, which can pose problems when using clays that are less plastic or heavily grogged.

Some manufactured dies come with fixed metal fittings so that the inner and outer sections of the die are held in permanent relationship to each other. Likewise, homemade hollow dies are fitted permanently together, often with U-bolts. The advantages to permanent fittings are obvious—there is no need to remove and clean the internal die holder between uses with different dies, saving you both time and work.

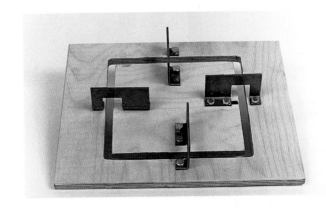

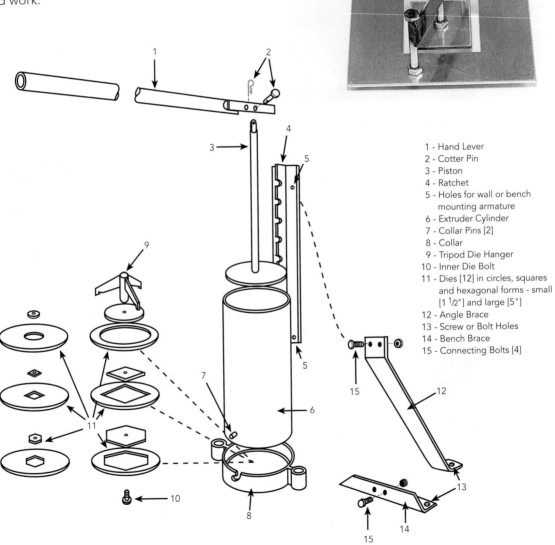

1 - Hand Lever
2 - Cotter Pin
3 - Piston
4 - Ratchet
5 - Holes for wall or bench
    mounting armature
6 - Extruder Cylinder
7 - Collar Pins [2]
8 - Collar
9 - Tripod Die Hanger
10 - Inner Die Bolt
11 - Dies [12] in circles, squares
    and hexagonal forms - small
    [1 1/2"] and large [5"]
12 - Angle Brace
13 - Screw or Bolt Holes
14 - Bench Brace
15 - Connecting Bolts [4]

This exploded drawing of a Randall extruder clearly shows the construction of a manual extruder—the barrel, plunger, handle, die holder, and back bar, as well as the internal die holder and dies.

EXPANSION BOXES

Most potters choose to use extruders fitted with these compact attachments, which increase the size of extrusions a standard studio extruder can make. Most expansion boxes are 9 inches (22.5 cm) square. The maximum extrusion possible from a 9-inch (22.5 cm) expansion box is about 8 inches (20 cm) and depends on how dies are fitted to the box. For some extruders, dies must be C-clamped to the expansion box; on others, dies are placed inside a die holder fastened to the edge of the expansion box, lessening the usable die area.

A 9-inch expansion box can extrude, among other things, a large, hollow cylinder.

GEAR-DRIVEN MANUAL EXTRUDERS

Hand-operated extruders can also be gear-driven, eliminating the need for back bars and long lever handles. A gear-driven manual extruder is constructed using some of the same components as other manual models, but is powered by a different principle. The barrel and plunger are the same, but instead of a lever pushing the clay though the tube, a gear does the work. The handle is round (like a steering wheel), and

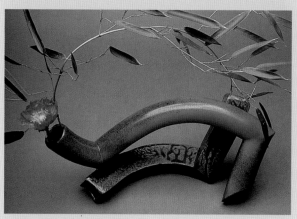

Top: FRANK BOSCO, *Untitled*, 1998. 9 x 11½ x 8 inches (22.5 x 28.75 x 20 cm), excluding floral arrangement. Stoneware; extruded and altered in one piece; cone 10 reduction. Floral arrangement by Yi-an Chou.
Bottom: FRANK BOSCO, *Vase*, 1998. 6 x 16 x 5 inches (15 x 40 x 12.5 cm) Stoneware; extruded and handbuilt; cone 10 reduction. Floral arrangement by Yi-an Chou.
Photos by Les Helmers.

the force used in turning it is transmitted to a gear that moves the plunger down the tube.

One of the benefits of not having a lever handle is safety. The lever can pinch fingers and accidentally swing down, hitting the operator's head. If a child is using a manual extruder, it's probably safest to use a gear-driven machine.

MOUNTING AND MAINTENANCE

MOUNTING

Whether handle-operated or gear-driven, with or without removable expansion boxes, most manual extruders are mounted vertically on a wall, column, or tabletop. The choice of wall or table mount may depend on the space available in your studio and the construction of its walls. It may be easier to table-mount the extruder than to fix it to a wall which is not strong enough or poses a difficult attachment. Some extruders table-mount easily, while others require a special fixture to accommodate mounting to a table. The clearance needed to use an extruder, especially one with an expansion box attached, is more easily accommodated by wall mounting.

Some extruders come with materials to fasten them to a wall or tabletop, and some even include materials for both options. Either way, mounting an extruder is a straightforward process—but one which should be done carefully, as an improperly mounted extruder can ruin the extruder, the surface on which it is mounted, the piece you're working on, and your day, if it comes loose from its moorings.

To wall-mount your extruder, first find the height at which you can comfortably load clay, operate the machine, and still have enough clearance from the bottom of the die to extrude a length of at least 2 feet (60 cm). Depending on your own height, a good distance from floor to extruder top should be between 4 and 5 feet (120 and 150 cm). Once you've got the position right, drill holes in the wall in appropriate locations determined by holes in the back bar, and bolt the back bar to the wall. (The type of fasteners required to firmly fix the extruder in place will be determined by the wall's construction.) Make sure the wall is solid—thick plywood, plaster with studs, or cement block are advisable. If the extruder has a removable expansion box, you may want to mount a thick piece of wood on the wall behind the back bar, so that there is adequate clearance between the wall and extruder to easily attach and remove the expansion box.

Table-mounting is easier. Again, it's important to choose a table or sturdy horizontal surface at the height that best accommodates the extrusion process. Make sure that the end of the barrel clears the table end to allow extrusions unfettered exit. If your extruder has legs, drill holes through the table that match the holes in the extruder legs. Place bolts through the holes in the extruder's legs and table and secure them with nuts and washers.

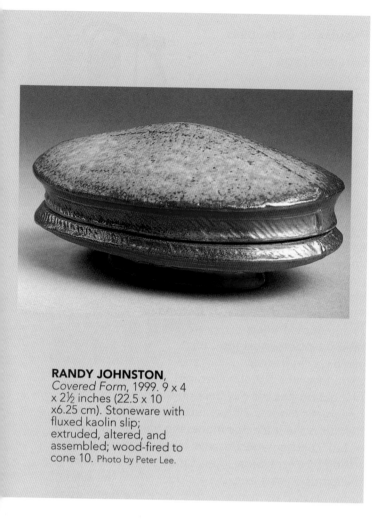

RANDY JOHNSTON, *Covered Form*, 1999. 9 x 4 x 2½ inches (22.5 x 10 x 6.25 cm). Stoneware with fluxed kaolin slip; extruded, altered, and assembled; wood-fired to cone 10. Photo by Peter Lee.

MAINTENANCE

Manual extruders don't need much in the way of maintenance, other than regular cleanings. Because clay left over from a previous use will dry out and adversely affect a new series of extrusions, all parts of the extruder in contact with clay should be cleaned after each use (or before the next use). Potters have come up with a number of preventative and after-use methods to keep extruder barrels clean, and you may devise your own. Meanwhile, here are some tips:

■ Before filling the extruder with clay, spray a thin film of non-stick vegetable spray, all-purpose spray petroleum lubricant, or a similar substance on the inside of the barrel, the plunger, and die holder.

■ After using the extruder, push a block of wood the size of your barrel wrapped in a scrap of old blue jean or other material through the barrel.

■ For square-barreled extruders, use a flat scraper to remove clay from inside walls.

OTHER TYPES OF EXTRUDERS: HAND-HELD, PNEUMATIC, MOTORIZED, AND HOMEMADE

HAND-HELD EXTRUDERS

If you've ever decorated a cake, squeezed threads of garlic through a press, plunked out cookies through a cookie press, or extruded squiggles with a child's toy for making clay shapes, you know that even the tiniest, least complicated extruder is fun to use. These diminutive extruders, designed for other purposes, can be adapted for use with clay that is soft, plastic, and finely grained. There are also a couple of commercially available, small, inexpensive, hand-operated tools that can be used with soft clay to create small forms or additions to larger works.

FINGER-OPERATED EXTRUDERS

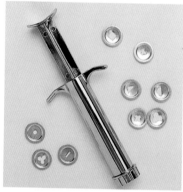

These aluminum tools, just 6 inches (15 cm) long, are held in the hand and worked like a hypodermic needle. Used with an assortment of ready-made dies, they are great for creating forms less than an inch (2.5 cm) in diameter in a variety of shapes to make millifiore inlay, jewelry, and other miniature items. Blank dies made of aluminum or plastic are provided for finger-operated extruders.

CLAY GUNS

Designed and worked like caulking guns, these small machines are good for tasks such as extruding lengths for coil and band building, handles, or decorative additions. They are easily cleaned with a brush or sponge.

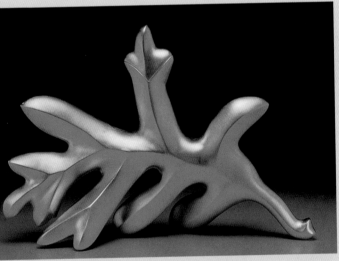

Top: MICHAEL SHERRILL, *Bloom Form*, 1998. Form on left: 16 x 12 x 4 inches (40 x 30 x 10 cm); form on right: 23 x 6 x 5 inches (57.5 x 15 x 12.5 cm). Stoneware; extruded and altered; metallic glaze; cone 05.

Bottom: MICHAEL SHERRILL, *Golden Leaf*, 1998. 14 x 18 x 5 inches (35 x 45 x 12.5 cm). Stoneware; extruded and altered with applied 23K gold leaf; cone 05. Photo by Tim Barnwell.

PNEUMATIC EXTRUDERS

Extruding large amounts of clay requires greater force. Because manual studio extruders have their limitations, some potters prefer extruders powered by air compressors. (Potters' studios often include air compression systems to power other tools such as spray guns and mixers, making pneumatic extrusion a viable alternative.)

Pneumatic extruders operate in somewhat the same way as manual extruders—the barrel is filled with clay and the plunger pushes the clay through the barrel. But for pneumatic models, air pressure, rather than a lever handle, is the force that moves the plunger. This offers a distinct advantage: Because the air pressure is controlled by a foot pedal, both hands are free to catch the extrusion as it exits the extruder. While the same items created by manual extrusion can be made using a pneumatic extruder, pneumatic power allows you to create larger extrusions when working alone.

MOTORIZED EXTRUDERS

Some potters' studios include a pugmill, which is most commonly used for mixing and recycling clay, and can also be used for extruding medium-sized

A Bluebird extruding nozzle can be fitted with internal baffles, as shown, to facilitate wider, flat extrusions.

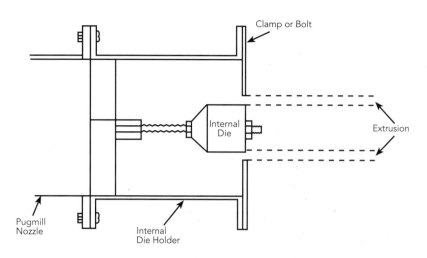

This diagram depicts the internal workings of a Bluebird Pugmill with an internal die holder and an accessory 4¼-inch (10.6 cm) round nozzle for extruding hollow shapes.

and larger forms. Pugmills are gear-driven and powered by an electric motor. They work somewhat differently than manual extruders. Moist clay is fed into a hopper (a container or opening) and pushed through the barrel by an auger (a rotating screw that drives material through a tube or pipe). Some pugmills are designed to extrude; some are not recommended for extrusion because of the problems of extruding clay with an auger. (Many are adapted to extrusion despite the difficulties). Two problems inherent in pugmill extrusion are auger memory and flow-speed differential. Auger memory refers to the auger's spiraling and the tendency of clay to retain in its structure the memory of this motion, which can cause S-cracking and other problems which sometimes aren't revealed until after firing.

Flow-speed problems can create extrusions which split and tear as they exit the machine. This is caused by the extruded clay coming out from the center of the nozzle and dies faster than from the sides. These difficulties can be solved by various retarders, or baffles, placed in strategic locations in the nozzle of the extruder—either on the walls or in the center. Pugmills used for extrusion require different or additional nozzles—one for tile extrusion, and another which is fitted with an internal die holder to extrude hollow forms.

Pugmills are usually made of steel and aluminum and come in a range of sizes and models, from a small tabletop model to a large pugmill that stands on the floor and delivers extrusions horizontally. Often, the auger and barrel are made of stainless steel or a combination of stainless steel and aluminum, to prevent rust from contaminating the clay. Pugmills are powerful machines and most commonly used to extrude tiles, tubes, and larger forms. Because they are heavy-duty machines, they are less appropriate for extruding smaller, more delicate forms.

Because mounting and maintenance requirements can vary depending on the size, weight, and construction of different

Motorized tile extruder from Radical Ridge Pottery

17

pugmills, it's important to carefully follow manufacturer's instructions. Cleaning the barrel of a pugmill is more or less difficult depending on the model and manufacturer.

Users of pugmill extruders make their own dies and usually recommend polyolefin plastics such as ultra-high-molecular-weight polyethylene (UHMW) or high-density polyethylene (HDPE), wood, or steel for use as die materials. UHMW and HDPE are strong and slippery materials, and facilitate clay sliding through the die. Polycarbonate is not recommended for pugmill extrusion as it is not sufficiently slippery. Before making plastic or metal dies, one manufacturer recommends practicing die-making with ½-inch (1.3 cm) plywood, because it is inexpensive and easy to work with.

HOMEMADE EXTRUDERS

Although many types of commercial extruders are available, many potters choose to design and construct their own machines from all manner of materials and powered by various means. For reasons of budget, specialized requirements, or the sheer fun of invention, some still opt for the homemade approach—with metal or plastic for barrels, or using various kinds of auto jacks for basic parts. Homemade extruders, depending on their size, materials, and mechanical makeup, have their own mounting and maintenance needs. Beginners may want to stick with a commercial extruder, but if you've been at it for awhile, or are particularly handy, here are some ideas from those who have done it their way.

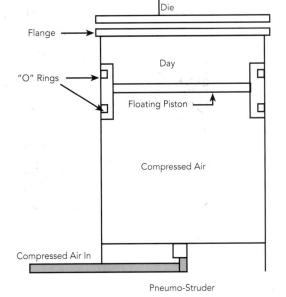

Nils Lou's pneumatic extruder, when oriented upright, can create large, hollow cylinders; when positioned horizontally, it can be converted for tile extrusion.

Pneumo-Struder

Above: *More than twenty years ago, a blacksmith made this extruder from an old Volkswagon car jack for Isak Isakkson. It holds 12 lbs. of clay.*

Left: *David Hendley, who lives and works in Maydelle, Texas, built his extruder (modeled after a Brent) in 1975. While he gathered materials for it at the junkyard, he also found an angled iron table frame on which he mounted the extruder.*

Jim Robison uses a homemade rectangular extruder to make wide base sections for his relief sculptures. *Photo by Simon Morley.*

Above and right: *Michael Sherrill designed and built this unique stainless steel power extruder, which can also revolve like a potter's wheel. Creating this homemade extruder was for Sherrill the result of wanting to be able to manipulate forms straight from the extruder; he designs his own dies specifically for this purpose. Photos by Tim Barnwell.*

Below: *Paul Stubbs built his deairing pugmill/extruder, patterned after a design by Harry Davis (in his book The Potter's Alternative), thirty-five years ago. This machine will make extrusions 10 inches (25 cm) wide.*

Pictured above is Lewis Snyder's extruder in action.

BASIC SETUP AND CLAY-WORKING TOOLS

(Note: The basic tools listed below comprise a general assortment that you will use for different aspects of creating clay works with extrusion. Tools and materials specific to individual projects are listed with the projects in each chapter.)

Making extruded work doesn't require a fancy high-tech studio. Other than your extruder, a sturdy surface on which to mount it, and tools to properly fix it to a table or wall, you will need some basic amenities and a handful of clayworking tools. Though you may decide to add power tools to your collection as your work with extrusion progresses, here's what you need to get started.

Clockwise from center: plastic bowl; spray bottle; hair dryer; toggle wire; pin tool; fettling knife; smooth and serrated metal ribs; harp; Surform tool; cheese wire; and sponges.

TOOLS

- A potter's knife, to cut clay.

- A craft knife with a razor-like blade, for cutting clay that is especially soft or thin, or for making especially refined cuts.

- A smooth metal rib, to smooth slabs or other clay surfaces.

- A serrated metal rib, for "roughing up" or scoring clay surfaces to prepare them for joining.

- A pin tool or "needle" tool, for more deeply scoring clay surfaces in preparation for joining.

- A wooden tool with one spoon-shaped end and one diagonally cut end, to help join and finish clay seams.

- A wooden rolling pin, to roll out clay slabs.

- A loop trimming tool, to carve designs in stiff clay.

- A Surform tool, for planing clay surfaces.

- A toggle wire, for cutting extrusions away from the extruder's barrel.

- A cheese wire, for delicate cutting, and a harp (a larger, taut wire) for cutting larger clay forms.

- Assorted bamboo brushes, for putting water on seams to be joined.

YOUR WORK AREA

- A work surface. A large, sturdy table or counter will work best.

- Ware boards. A few pieces of plywood (12 x 24 inches [30 x 60 cm], or 18 x 24 inches [45 x 60 cm]) on which to move clay constructions, and a few long, thin boards (½ x 4 x 24 inches [1.3 x 10 x 60 cm]) for carrying extrusions.

- Plastic bats. A couple of round, plastic surfaces on which to build and move clay constructions.

Top: WALTER KEELER, *Sauce Boat*, 1998. 15 x 18 x 11 inches (37.5 x 45 x 27.5 cm). White earthenware; form and base thrown and altered, handle extruded; bisque fired to cone 01.
Bottom: WALTER KEELER, *Tripod Bowl*, 1997. 8¼ x 7½ x 7½ inches (21 x 19 x 19 cm). Stoneware; form thrown, legs extruded, cut, and bent; salt glazed, cone 10. Photos by artist.

■ Sheets of canvas. Canvas is the best material to use to cover your worktable; you'll also need a piece or two for rolling and flipping clay slabs.

■ Sponges. You'll want a small sponge for working with clay, and a large one for cleanup.

■ A spray water bottle. This will come in handy for misting clay to keep it moist while you're working.

■ Plastic bowls. Have a couple in different sizes on hand to hold water to dampen or wet clay constructions and mix plaster.

■ Plastic garbage bags, or dry cleaner plastic. Wrapping clay in these while you work on other parts of a project or construction will keep the clay from drying out. You can also wrap finished projects or constructions in plastic while they're drying later on.

■ A hair dryer. This will help to stiffen clay parts.

SAFETY

Manual extruders aren't dangerous. The handle or lever, however, can surprise you and fall unexpectedly from an upright position, so make sure to keep your head out of its striking range! There are also a few pinch points on lever-handled extruders—where the handle pivots, and where the plunger enters the barrel—so be sure to work carefully around these parts. Electrically powered pugmills, on the other hand, can be quite dangerous. Exercise all caution when the machine is turned on, keeping your hands away from the hopper and moving blades. Likewise, when you're using power tools to make dies, it is important to dress appropriately. Wear protective clothing and equipment when drilling, sawing, or grinding—safety glasses, long sleeves, and gloves are advisable. When drilling dies, make sure the die is clamped securely to the table. When grinding plastic with a motorized tool, wear long sleeves and cotton gloves to protect from tiny bits of hot plastic that are thrown off. Whenever you are using a motorized piece of equipment or tool, carefully follow the manufacturer's instructions and precautions.

CHAPTER TWO

DIES: READY-MADE, CUSTOM, AND MAKING YOUR OWN

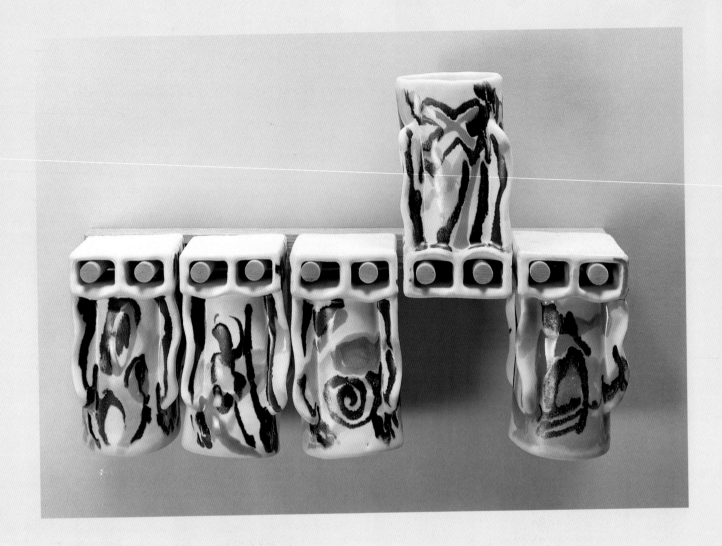

JOHN H. STEPHENSON,
Extruded Cups on Wall Rack, 1998.
9½ x 15 x 4⅜ inches (23.75 x 37.5 x
10.9 cm); individual cups each 5½ x
3⅜ x 2⅞ inches (13.75 x 8.4 x 7.2
cm). White stoneware; extruded
and altered; single glaze fire after
bisque; cone 6. Photo by artist.

CHOOSING MATERIALS

Like ready-mades, homemade dies can be constructed of various materials, and choosing the right one depends to some extent on which materials you are comfortable working with. Most manufacturers sell die blanks made of the same materials as their ready-made dies—plastic, aluminum, or wood (often Baltic birch or cabinet-grade plywood)—and some also sell the hardware to hold together the inner and outer parts of hollow dies. You can also buy materials from other sources and make the die from scratch. Quality plywoods, metals, and plastics of various types and thicknesses can be used.

PLASTIC

Certain plastics are optimal for making dies. Most are sold by the square foot (cut to your request) or at reduced prices in oddly shaped scraps. Only some plastics will work for making dies—the material must be strong enough to withstand the force of clay being pressed against it. I prefer to use ¼-inch-thick (6 mm) polycarbonate plastic to make dies for my 4-inch (10 cm) extruder because it is inexpensive, strong even when thin, easy to work with, and can be cut and finished with common woodworking tools.

The following plastics purchased in suggested thicknesses also work well and are commonly used for making dies: polyolefins such as ⅜-inch-thick (9 mm) ultra-high-molecular-weight polyethylene (UHMW) and high-density polyethylene (HDPE); and ¼- or ⅜-inch (6 or 9 mm) polyformaldehyde (Delrin). They all have tough, chemically resistant surfaces, and an additional advantage—they are slippery, which facilitates extrusion. Potters who extrude large quantities of tile prefer the slippery qualities of UHMW and HDPE dies and do not recommend polycarbonate. Also, because the polyolefins are not as rigid as polycarbonates, they must be used at greater thicknesses. But they have good working properties—

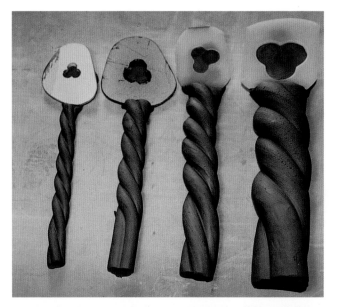

David Hendley created these dies for decorative ropes and bands. Twisting the beaded extrusion adds an interesting variation.

with normal woodworking tools, they can be cut and ground to produce dies with fine, smooth edges.

I have not found it necessary to reinforce 4-inch (10 cm) round ¼-inch-thick (6 mm) polycarbonate dies used with soft clay, but larger plastic dies, or small dies made from thin or low-quality plastic, may need to be reinforced to withstand pressure from the clay. To reinforce plastic dies, you can attach ⅜-inch-thick (9 mm) plywood to the bottom side of the die, or sandwich the plastic between two pieces of ¼-inch-thick (6 mm) plywood. These wooden supports can be cut to match the outside diameter of the die and attached to the plastic using ¼-inch (6 mm) hexagonal nuts and bolts. Die profiles cut in the supports must be larger than those in the die, to prevent interference with the extrusion.

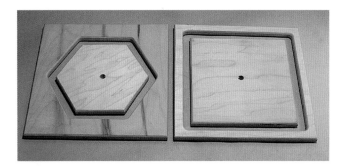

WOOD

If you prefer to use wood to make your dies, ½-inch-thick (1.3 cm) cabinet-grade or Baltic birch plywood are good choices—they're inexpensive, and easy to cut and finish with normal woodworking tools. Exterior-grade Baltic birch plywood, which is stronger than standard plywoods because of increased laminations per inch and the nature of the wood itself, will withstand exposure to wet clay over time. Cabinet-grade plywood, while not designed for exterior use, has more laminations than standard plywoods (five instead of three), and also holds up well to the force of clay pressing against it. It is a stock item in most lumberyards, and so is more readily available than Baltic birch, which usually has to be special ordered.

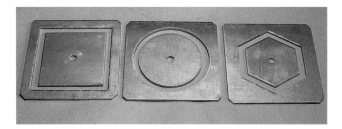

METAL

Making metal dies is more difficult than making dies from plastic or wood. While metal dies may have a longer life, plastic is still probably a better choice for most beginning die makers. But if you have some experience with metalworking, and have or don't mind buying the proper equipment—drill bits, saws, and files—you can make dies with16-gauge steel (about 1/16 inch [1.5 mm] thick). Brass (¼ inch [6 mm] thick) or aluminum (⅛ to 3/16 inch [3 to 5 mm] thick) can also be used, but cutting them will probably require professional metal machining equipment.

If you choose to make your own steel dies, you'll need a coping saw with a coarse blade for cutting. (Because of the metal's thinness, it doesn't need to be bevel edged.) You can also get sheet steel laser-cut for a fee, but the charge for set up for a single die tends to be prohibitive.

Top: DIANA PANCIOLI, *Bed I.*, 1988. 3 x 6 feet (90 x 180 cm); extruded components each 3 x 8 inches (7.5 x 20 cm). Low-fire white clay with terra sigilatta; extruded and altered (suspended with nylon monofilament); cone 04.

Bottom: DIANA PANCIOLI, *Deathbed*,1988. 3 x 3 feet (90 x 90 cm); extruded components each 3 x 8 inches (7.5 x 20 cm). Low-fire white clay with black terra sigilatta and translucent low-fire clay; extruded and altered, with upper components slab-built and fired in biscuit molds (suspended with nylon monofilament); cone 04. Photos by artist.

PROJECT
PLASTIC DIES PROJECT

(Note: The following tools, materials, and instructions are specific to making a plastic die. If you choose to make a die from plywood or other material, you can follow the same general process with appropriate adaptations.)

ALONG WITH A STURDY WORK SURFACE, YOU'LL NEED THE FOLLOWING MATERIALS AND TOOLS TO MAKE YOUR DIE:

¼-INCH-THICK (6 MM) POLYCARBONATE (OR OTHER PLASTIC IN SUGGESTED THICKNESS) THE SIZE OF YOUR DIE HOLDER OR EXPANSION BOX

DIE DRAWING

MASKING TAPE (IF USING PLASTIC OTHER THAN POLYCARBONATE)

½-INCH-THICK (1.3 CM) PIECE OF SCRAP WOOD

220-, 400, AND 600-GRIT SANDPAPER (OPTIONAL)

RULER

PENCIL OR MARKER

C-CLAMP OR VISE

HACKSAW WITH 18-TOOTH BLADE

COPING SAW OR JEWELER'S SAW WITH COARSE BLADE

JIGSAW (OPTIONAL)

BAND SAW (OPTIONAL)

DRILL

AN ASSORTMENT OF BITS

ASSORTED FILES IN VARIOUS SIZES*

HAND-HELD MOTORIZED GRINDING TOOL WITH HIGH-SPEED CUTTING BITS*

(Note: Ordinary hand files work well to bevel and refine interior die edges. A round and half-round bastard file from the local hardware store will work for dies with openings larger than the dimension of the files. Smaller openings will require smaller files. An inexpensive kit of mixed files is worth the small cost. A hand-held motorized grinding tool used with metal cutting bits works quickly to help shape and bevel plastic. Rotating at 5 to 30 thousand rpms, the best speed for grinding plastic is about 15 to 20 thousand.)

The die-making tools and supplies pictured here are (clockwise): a motorized jig saw; polycarbonate plastic die blanks; a coping saw and blades; a hacksaw; U-bolts and nuts; large and small files; an electric drill and bits; a C-clamp; and motorized hand tool and cutting bits.

A Solid Die

(Note: If your extruder's die holder is square, step 1 may be bypassed by having a plastic supplier cut die-sized pieces of plastic for a small charge.)

1 Measure the internal dimensions of your extruder's die holder, and select a slightly larger piece of plastic. Transfer your die drawing onto the plastic. The drawn shape, which when cut will be your die, must be small enough to drop easily into the die holder, but large enough to be well supported all around by the interior edge of the die holder. Holding the plastic steady with a C-clamp or vise, use a band saw, jigsaw, hacksaw, or coping saw to cut the exterior shape. (A handsaw can cut HDPE, Delrin, and polycarbonate fairly quickly; in about 10 minutes, you can cut two sides of a 5-inch [12.5 cm] square from a sheet. UHMW is also easy to cut by hand, but takes longer.)

2 If you're using polycarbonate, transfer the die hole shape you have designed onto the paper covering the plastic. Other plastics don't include this paper covering; you'll need to cover one face of the die with masking tape, then transfer your design onto the tape.

3 Next, place a ½-inch-thick (1.3 cm) scrap wood board on your work surface. Position the blank plastic die on top of the board with the drawing face up, and use a C-clamp to tightly fasten the plastic and board to the tabletop.

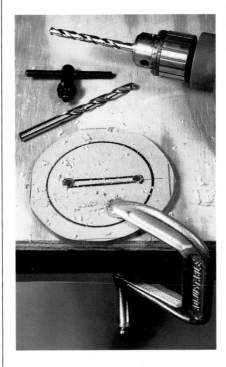

4 Drill two or three holes inside your drawn profile—at the ends and center of the shape, or at points that are appropriate for the particular die shape you are making. (Some solid dies are made entirely by drilling, with careful placement of variously sized bits.)

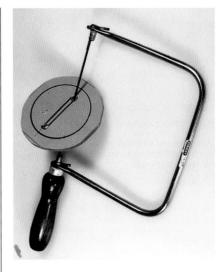

5 Holding the die with a vise or clamp, insert the blade of a coping saw, jeweler's saw, or jigsaw, into one of the drilled holes, and cut from hole to hole along the marked lines. (Don't worry if the cut isn't perfect—you will bevel and refine the profile later.)

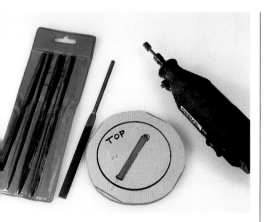
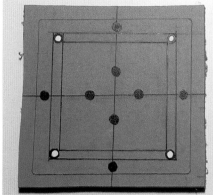
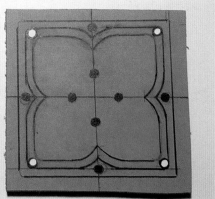

6 Choose one side of the die to serve as the bottom and clearly mark the other side "top". Using a hand file or hand-held motorized grinding tool, file or grind the topside of the die profile to a bevel angled between 20 and 45°. The contour of the die's topside profile will be a larger, more open, and less exact profile than the bottom contour. The die's bottom-side profile will be the exact shape you want the clay extrusion to take. Beveling the topside profile allows more clay to enter the die. The die opening works like a funnel: Clay is squeezed and its shape defined as it is forced down through the die thickness into its final form, moving from the larger, less defined contour through a tighter, more exact one.

7 Once the die is bevelled, refine and smooth the edges with files or sandpaper until you are satisfied with the results. *(Note: One power extruder user recommends finishing die edges with 220-, 400-, and 600-grit sandpapers. Power extrusion requires more refined die edges than manual extrusion. Although edges can be heat-polished, the strength and resiliency of some plastics are degraded by heat. If you choose to heat-polish your die, first make sure that the plastic you're using is suited to this method.)*

A HOLLOW DIE

(Note: In addition to the materials and tools listed above for making a solid die, you'll need a few U-bolts ¼ to ⁵⁄₁₆ inch [6 to 8 mm] thick x 1 to 2 inches [2.5 to 5 cm] long, and some nuts to make your hollow die.)

Planning a hollow die requires an extra step—estimating where your die will need U-bolt support. A die for hollow extrusion must include a device to hold the center profile in place. Simple U-bolts from the hardware store work well to span the space between the outer die segment and the center profile. Clay flows around the U-bolts and heals into a hollow form as it exits the die.

U-bolt placement can be tricky. Start by making marks for U-bolt placement on your die face, spacing the U-bolts evenly around the die for maximum support (three or more depending on the size of the die) and as perpendicular as possible to the

die's profile. If you position the U-bolts at angles, the die can twist over time, altering the spacing which creates the extrusion's wall. Make certain that distances between the U-bolt legs are accurate and that you leave clearances for the nuts which will hold them in place. The outer legs of all U-bolts and their nuts must clear the die holder hole; the nuts must not impinge on the external die holder rim, or on each other where they come together in the center of the die. To make a hollow die:

1 Follow steps 1 through 3 for Making A Solid Die.

2 Drill holes for U-bolt supports as indicated by your drawing.

3 Using a drill bit the width of your die walls, drill three or four holes at locations where the drawn shape turns corners. Sharp corners are more difficult to extrude, so the round drilled holes at corners of the die profile facilitate a good extrusion.

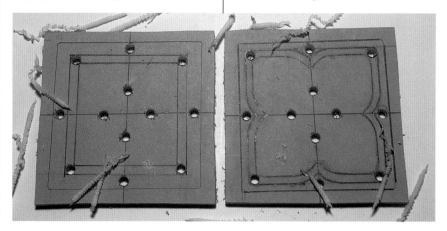

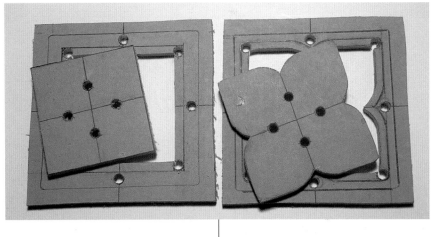

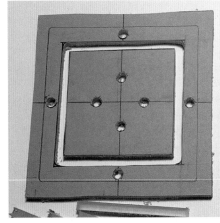

4 Next, holding the die steady with a vise or clamp, use a coping saw or jigsaw to cut from hole to hole along the drawn profile closest to the center of the die. The center portion that you cut out first will provide the block-out shape for your die, creating the hole in your extrusion. Set this piece aside for now.

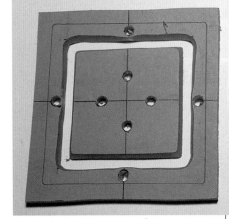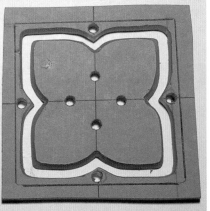

5 Cut the second, outer line of the die profile. You will be cutting away the wall thickness which, for a small die, is usually ¼ to ⅜ inch (6 to 9 mm).

6 Using a hand file or hand-held motorized grinding tool, file or grind the topsides of both parts of your die profile to a bevel angled between 20 and 45°. The contour of the die's topside profile will be a larger, more open, and less exact profile than the bottom contour.

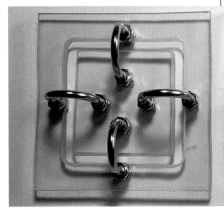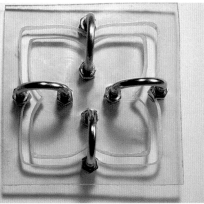

7 Once the edges are filed to your satisfaction, you're ready to assemble the die. Screw hex nuts onto the U-bolt legs about ½ inch (1.3 cm) from their tips (the plastic thickness plus the thickness of one hex nut). Next, place the U-bolts through the topsides of the plastic die parts; screw the hex nuts onto the U-bolt's legs where they come through the bottom side of the die. All U-bolts should be screwed into the bottom nuts evenly,

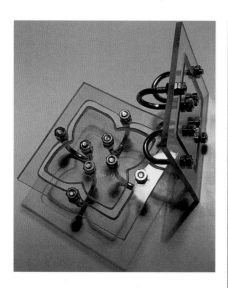

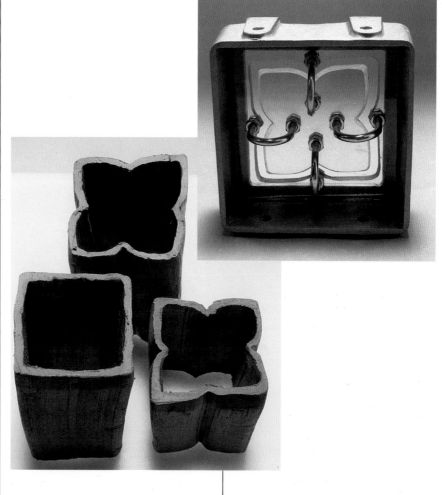

with their threaded ends not protruding but just level with their nuts' bottom sides. Adjust the plastic downward to this placement and screw the topside nuts downward to the plastic. This process will insure that the center of the die is level with the outer section. If the two parts of the die, the inner and outer forms, do not remain level in relationship to each other when the form is extruded, the extrusion will bend. Now your die is ready to use.

CHAPTER THREE

CLAY BODIES AND EXTRUSION

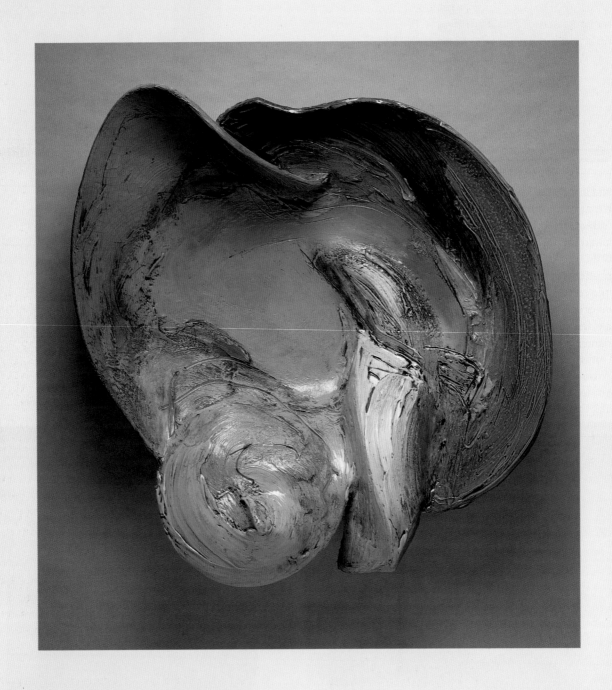

SUSANNE STEPHENSON, *Dusk VI*, 1997. 27½ x 26 x 8½ inches (68.75 x 65 x 21.25 cm). Terra-cotta; thrown rim with extruded hollow forms, slab base; cone 03. Photo by John Stepehenson.

PEOPLE HAVE BEEN WORKING with clay for millennia, making objects for everyday use and items for enjoyment and ritual events—bowls and storage jars, jewelry and ornaments, effigies and burial urns. In the beginning, potters used clay straight from their surrounding environments, dug from the earth. Over time, they discovered that adding a gritty tempering material, such as sand, allowed their work to dry without cracking and fire with less breakage.

Around the ninth century A.D., potters discovered that they could make composite bodies with specific desired properties—for example, lighter fired colors, different textures, or particular firing temperatures. By formulating bodies of various clays combined with other materials, they could create wares more closely in tune with their needs and desires. This technical shift from clay to clay body marked an important advance in the development of ceramics, and is an important distinction when discussing clays and clay bodies.

Before you begin making extruded work, you'll need to know about available types of generic clays, and which ones are best to use to formulate clay bodies for extrusion. Like other forms of claywork, the demands of extrusion make certain clay bodies optimal for the process (although a good throwing body will probably also extrude well). Along with giving

some general information on the natures of different clays, this chapter will familiarize you with clay bodies best used for extrusion. It also offers advice about qualities to look for if you are purchasing ready-made bodies to extrude with, and some troubleshooting tips to help solve problems you may encounter in extrusion process.

CLAYS

Clays fall into a few major categories, divided by geologists according to the ways in which the clays were originally formed. The following is a list of the major families of clay, their general characteristics, and what these qualities impart to a clay body formula.

■ Fire clays mature at high temperatures. They are relatively pure, buff to medium in fired color, and often coarse-grained and nonplastic. Fire clays are crushed to various mesh sizes; smaller mesh fire clays are more plastic.

■ Kaolins are high-temperature china clays. They are very pure, buff to white in fired color, fine- to medium-grained, and usually nonplastic (some are more plastic than others).

■ Stoneware clays mature at medium temperatures, are somewhat impure, fire from buff to a medium color, and are usually fine grained and plastic.

KATHY DAMBACH, *White Squared Balance*, 1990. 28 x 28 x 10 inches (70 x 70 x 25 cm). Sttoneware and low-fire white clays; extruded and altered.

- Ball clays fire to medium temperature, are somewhat impure, have a buff to medium fired color, and are fine grained and plastic.

- Red clays (terra-cottas) mature at lower temperatures. They are dark and impure, orange to brown in fired color, medium-grained, and can vary in plasticity.

FORMULATING A CLAY BODY FOR EXTRUSION

You can construct a body specifically for extrusion, but its formula will not vary greatly from those used for wheel-throwing. A clay body for extrusion must do all the things a standard body does—be sufficiently plastic, dry without cracking, shrink the right amount, and mature at the chosen temperature. Most clay bodies will extrude if they are plastic enough and of the right softness.

Extruded work can be made with every kind of clay body, from high- and medium-temperature stoneware and porcelain to low-temperature whiteware and terra-cotta. Bodies for extrusion can be purchased from a supplier or constructed from a formula.

If you make a body specifically for extrusion, you must remember that all parts of the final object should be constructed from the same clay body— extrusions, slabs, thrown parts, additions, etc. Shrinkage differences will cause problems if you try to combine parts extruded from one body with parts made from a different body.

The specific clays you choose for your body formula will depend on the temperature at which you wish to fire the work, the qualities you want your body to have, and the purposes for which you plan to use it. For a general-purpose body at any temperature, it is always a good idea to mix grain sizes (fire clays, stonewares, and ball clays, for instance). Too much fine-grained clay can cause drying and cracking problems; too much coarse-grained clay will make the body less plastic and more difficult to work with.

A clay body used for extrusion must be sufficiently plastic, and there are a number of ways to increase plasticity. A body can be made easier to extrude, for example, by increasing its percentage of plastic clays and by using the most plastic versions of usually non-plastic clays (fire clay, for instance). While bodies for extrusion should contain a percentage of ball clay as a component, do not add excessively large percentages. A body with too much ball clay will be flabby

and won't stiffen or dry normally, making the extrusions more difficult to handle. Choose other clays for your formula considering their plasticity; select the fire clays, kaolins, and stoneware clays that are more plastic than others.

You can also enhance the plasticity of bodies you're constructing by adding plasticizers. Bentonite or Veegum T, for example, added in amounts of 1 percent or less, will increase plasticity (more than this may

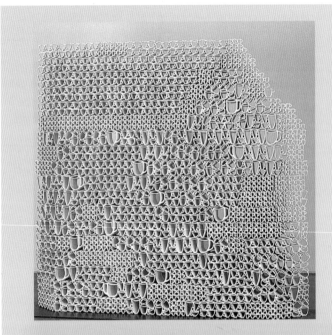

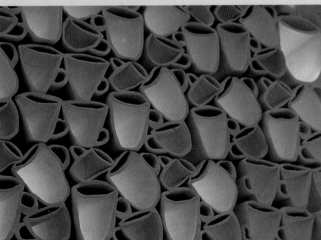

Top: INGE PEDERSON, *New Function*, 1998. 84 x 80 x 12 inches (210 x 200 x 30 cm). Stoneware; extruded modules (about 400, each 5½ x 5½ inches [13 x 13 cm]).
Bottom: INGE PEDERSON, *Blue Tradition*, 1998. 72 x 68 x 8 inches (180 x 170 x 20 cm). Stoneware; extruded modules (about 300, each 5½ x 5½ inches [13 x 13 cm]). Photos by Terje Agnalt.

cause problems). Organic ingredients such as beer, flour, and vinegar can also add to the plasticity of clay. Whether you add one of these ingredients may depend on how much you mind if your clay smells funny or grows molds.

In addition to clays and plasticizers, bodies are formulated with additives. These fall into two categories: fluxes and fillers. Fluxes make the body more vitreous (dense) and help the glaze bond to the body surface. Fillers assist the body in drying without cracking; fillers are the "tempering" ingredients such as sand or grog (crushed fire brick). Neither fluxes nor fillers contribute to the plasticity of the body.

The firing temperatures of different clay bodies determine which fluxes to use in them. Feldspars are most often used for high-temperature bodies. Talc, gerstley borate, frits, or softer feldspars are used for low-temperature bodies. Feldspars are complex minerals ground to fine powders that melt in a range from 2100 to 2400°F (1149 to 1350°C), with nepheline syenite, a softer feldspar, melting at the lower end of that range. Frits are industrially formulated glasses ground to fine powder. Lead-free frits melt at a wide range of temperatures, from 1400°F (760°C) to over 2000°F (1093°C), and are selected for use according to their melting temperature and formula. The mineral talc begins to melts at about 1650°F (899°C), and gerstley borate at around 1100°F (593°C). Fluxes are added to bodies in varying amounts from 0 to about 15 percent—some terra-cotta bodies need no fluxes at all, whereas porcelains are often formulated with a lot of flux to make them especially vitreous.

Sand is a cheap and available filler, but not good for high-temperature bodies where it can cause problems. Grog, though more expensive, is usually the filler of choice. It comes in graded grain sizes and is stable at all temperatures. Calcined fire clay is also sometimes used as an economical substitute for grog. Other grogs such as kyanite and mullite (calcined kyanite) come in various mesh sizes at about the same cost as calcined fire clay.

Fillers such as these used in general-purpose bodies are added in amounts from 0 to 12 percent. The purpose for which you will use your clay body will determine the amount of filler you add to it. Sculpture bodies, which are designed to be used at greater thickness, can include as much as 25 percent filler, and may not extrude well. Extruding bodies are usually formulated with less filler, from 0 to 8 percent, to achieve a smoother extruded surface.

Formulae

Below are some sample formulae. These are standard formulae with a few minor adjustments for extruding (1 percent of bentonite has been added). Stoneware, fire clays, and kaolins have been selected for plasticity. While these specific clays may not be available in your area, you can choose similar substitutes. These bodies should be made to a soft throwing consistency and aged. Plasticity can be enhanced by adding wet reclaimed clay (of the same formula) to the mixer batch. Reclaimed clay is overly wetted and already somewhat aged, augmenting plasticity and the body's ability to extrude.

Stoneware

Cone 10

Ingredient	Percentage
#6 tile kaolin	20
Edgar plastic kaolin	20
OM #4 ball clay	10
Hawthorne bond	15
Gold art stoneware	15
Custer feldspar	12
Flint	8
	100
Plus fine grog	8
Bentonite	1

Porcelain

Cone 10

Ingredient	Percentage
Grolleg	40
Edgar plastic kaolin	25
Tennessee 5 ball clay	10
Custer feldspar	15
Flint	10
	100
Plus fine molochite	5
Bentonite	1

Terra-Cotta

Cone 04

INGREDIENT	PERCENTAGE
Red art clay	50
Gold art stoneware	25
OM #5 ball clay	20
Talc	5
	100
Plus fine grog	8
Bentonite	1

To summarize, if you are formulating your own clay body for extrusion as well as for other methods of construction, you can increase its plasticity by:

■ Increasing the amount of ball clay in it by a few percent

■ Selecting fire clays, kaolins, and stonewares that are more plastic (finer-mesh fire clay)

■ Keeping the grog content at 8 percent or less

■ Using fine grog, or a mixture of fine and medium (not coarse)

■ Adding bentonite or Veegum T in amounts of 1 percent or less

■ Adding a small amount of an organic ingredient such as beer, vinegar, or flour

■ Mixing the clay so that it is wetter than usual—a soft throwing consistency that is soft, but not sticky

■ Using reclaimed clay which is already aged and plastic as part of the mixture

■ Aging the body for several months

COMMERCIALLY PREPARED CLAY BODIES

Clay bodies for extrusion are similar to all-purpose bodies, which is why most all-purpose bodies can be used for extrusion with just a few adjustments. Before purchasing ready-made clay bodies for extrusion, ask your supplier for his or her recommendations. He or she can suggest which body might be better for extrusion—those with a slightly higher percentage of plastic clays, for example, or those which that supplier makes softer. Some clay suppliers control the water content of their clays and offer variations—soft, medium, and stiff.

If you've been working with a particular clay body that fits your glazes and fires at the temperature and in the atmosphere you've chosen, you may want to stick with it as you add extrusion to your construction repertoire. In most cases, a few adjustments for consistency (wetness) and aging will make clays good for extruding; most bodies will extrude if they are soft enough and aged to increase their plasticity. Even if your clay body doesn't look like an extruding body—if, for example, it's especially groggy—give it a try. You might like what happens. Some potters purposely extrude groggy bodies for the ragged quality of the extrusions they produce. Purchased clay ages in the bag, which will increase its plasticity—but it may also become too stiff to extrude. If your boxed clay becomes too stiff, add a cup (8 oz.) of water to it (while it's still in the bag), reseal the plastic bag, and wait a week or so. Wedge it well (see Working With Clay, page 39) before using.

BODIES FOR EXTRUSION WITH MOLDMAKING

If you want to make plaster molds from extruded parts, you can make a clay body specifically for this purpose—one that extrudes very smoothly, but that you do not plan to fire. Simply dry out your reclaimed wet clay with additions of plastic clays—for example, ½ ball clay and ½ stoneware (do not add grog). Reclaimed clay slop is already aged and plastic from being over wetted. Additions of plastic clays will further enhance its plasticity and the body will extrude like a dream, making smooth and perfect extrusions, but it will be useful only for moldmaking. It will not fire well, dry without cracking, or fit your glazes. Remember to keep special formulations of clay for moldmaking separate from your regular clay body.

WORKING WITH CLAY

Whether you purchase a clay body or formulate one yourself, it will behave much the same way and require much the same treatment. Wedging—which evens out the moisture content of clay and eliminates air bubbles— is an important first step in preparing clay for making work, whether it is to be thrown, rolled, or extruded. It is best done on a cement, plaster, or canvas surface, one which the clay will not stick to. One wedging technique consists of kneading the clay with a rocking and spiraling motion which moves the inside clay to the outside. Air bubbles are squashed against the table surface, and the clay becomes mixed and homogenous. Beginners can wedge by simply banging the clay repeatedly on the table or work surface.

THE STAGES OF WORKING AND DRYING

Extruded clay goes through the same stages of drying as work made by throwing, handbuilding, or other clay-working techniques. First the clay is soft and plastic, but upon exposure to air becomes stiffer by degrees until it is finally dry. Developing a sensitivity to the various stages in the continuum from plastic to

Top: WILLIAM SHINN, *Fenestrated Form*, 1992. 17 x 23 x 8 inches (42.5 x 57.5 x 20 cm). White stoneware; extruded and carved; cone 10. Photo by artist.
Bottom: JOHN VAN ECK, *Cube*, 1998. 14 x 14 x 14 inches (35 x 35 x 35 cm). Glazed terra-cotta; extruded and assembled.

dry is important in creating all clay work, and is equally important when making extruded work.

Although there are only three stages of wetness/dryness in the potter's lexicon—plastic, leather-hard, and dry (or bone dry which means completely dry)—there are actually more. Leather-hard could be subdivided at least twice into flexible leather-hard and stiff leather-hard. Various steps in the clayworking process are best done when the clay is in different leather-hard stages, but the subtleties of stiffness are so difficult to describe they are usually just lumped under the term "leather-hard". Nevertheless, with experience you will develop an awareness of the wider differences, and learn to use this knowledge to advantage in making your work.

Potters use a number of techniques to delay the drying of clay work and hold it at workable leather-hard stages. Wrapping work in a layer or two of plastic sheeting can delay drying while allowing the work to "cure" to a leather-hard state. Likewise, misting work with a spray bottle can delay drying and maintain the softness and workability of extruded parts. Before being fired for the first time, clay work, including extruded work, should be "bone dry"—lighter in color, and not cold or damp to the touch.

FIRING EXTRUDED CLAY

Firing extruded clay work differs hardly at all from firing clay work made by other methods. If you are starting to work with extrusion, you more likely than not have experience with kilns and firing methods; any basic book on ceramics will provide complete information. The first firing, to chemically change clay to a permanently hard state, is called bisque or biscuit firing. At this stage, the ware is usually unglazed but may be decorated with colored slips which do not vitrify (become glassy). The bisque firing is usually lower in temperature than the later glaze firing. After the bisque fire, the piece is glazed or otherwise surfaced and returned to the kiln for a higher-temperature firing—the glaze fire.

In the bisque fire, the only difference that you must be concerned about when firing an extruded work is if it has enclosed hollow spaces, such as hollow handles or feet, which can trap steam. There are three ways to take care of this potential problem. If you dry the work very well, you should be able to avoid it altogether. Or you can make a tiny hole in each enclosed hollow space (a hole made by a pin tool is large enough). Most important, fire the bisque slowly in its early stages when steam is forming. Make certain that

pieces with hollow spaces are thoroughly dry after glazing, and fire them a little more slowly through the early part of the firing.

SURFACING EXTRUDED WORK

The type of work you are making, whether functional or sculptural, and your own surface preferences and skills with glaze materials, will determine how you finish the works you create with extrusion. Extruded work, like any other clay work, can be surfaced with slip, vitreous engobes, terra sigillata, maiolica, glazes that are dry, satin, matte, crusty, glossy, and so on. Functional considerations apply if you are making work to be used with food—non-toxic, washable surfaces are imperative. Sculptural work allows more freedom of surface treatments.

TROUBLESHOOTING: PROBLEMS, CAUSES, AND FIXES

Even ceramicists who have been using extruders for a long time run into problems. The following section deals with some of the more common pitfalls of the extrusion process, and how to avoid these problems or solve them once they are encountered.

Problem: The extrusion has a torn, rather than a smooth, surface. A torn surface looks rough, like tree bark. There are various degrees of tearing—from slightly rough to very rough with pieces lifted and holes formed. The following are possible causes and solutions:

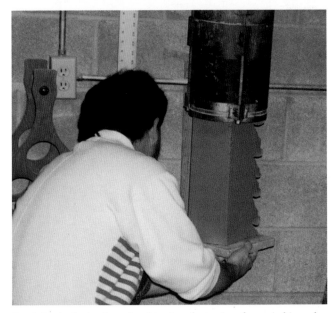

Lewis Snyder invites intentional tearing of extrusions for use in his work. He offsets the die slightly to catch a corner of the extrusion on the die holder as it exits the extruder.

- The die might not be bevelled enough .
  Increase the bevel angle.

- The die might be in the holder upside down.
  Turn it over.

- The corners of the die might be too sharp.
  Round the corners with a file.

- The clay might not be sufficiently aged.
  Store it longer before use.

- The clay isn't plastic.
  Reformulate your clay body ,increasing plastic clays or adding synthetic plasticizers. Or, if you're using purchased clay, try a different clay body.

- The clay might not be soft enough.
  If you are using purchased clay, add water to the clay, reseal the bag, and wait. Then re-wedge the clay.

- Your dies aren't slippery enough.
  Use a slipperier material , such as HDPE or Delrin, for your dies, or file and sand the dies.

- Flow forces within the extruding tube are having a negative effect.
  This is the oddest problem but natural to the extrusion process. Clay flows faster through the center of

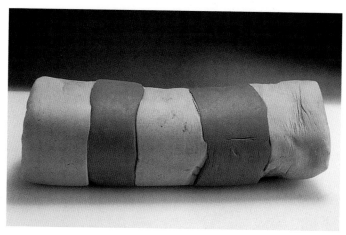

To create a visual image of clay flow in an extruder, light and dark clays are layered together before putting the pug into the extruder.

Early in the extruding process, the layered pug is taken from the barrel and wire-cut open to show the pattern of clay flowing faster through the center of the barrel.

FRANK BOSCO, *Olympus Mons*, 1999. 12 x 14 x 10 inches (30 x 35 x 25 cm). Stoneware; extruded; cone 10 reduction. Photo by artist.

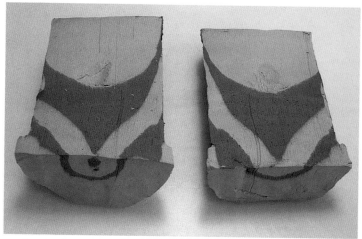

Further along in the extrusion process, the layered clay clearly shows the flow of clay in the barrel, with the center moving faster than the rest.

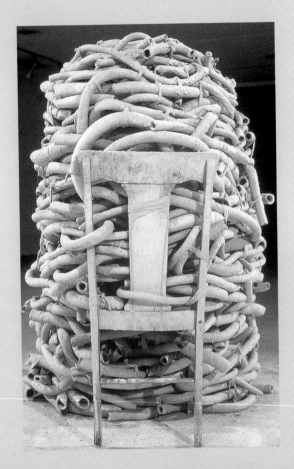

the barrel than down the sides. One reason for this speed differential is drag caused by clay sticking to the sides of the barrel. The second is that the die is allowing the clay out through the center of the barrel—no force is holding the clay back at that point. The flow pattern set in place during the emptying of the extruder barrel often has a negative effect on subsequent extrusions. The clay remaining at the bottom of the barrel causes the problem, but the solution is simple. When you notice that the first full barrel of clay extrudes well but upon reloading the extrusion begins to tear badly, try this:

Empty the barrel of all clay, especially the waste amount left just above the die (no need to clean the die), Re-wedge the clay and reload the barrel. This usually corrects the problem. Emptying the barrel will correct a different problem which also causes tearing. The clay on the top surface of the first pug, just below the plunger, often dries out. After you have extruded the first full tube of clay, remove the plunger and feel the clay inside the barrel to discover whether a crust has formed on top of the pug. This crusty layer will cause tearing if you put a new soft pug of clay on top of it and try to extrude. Instead, remove all the remaining clay, and use a new freshly wedged pug of clay.

Problem: The extrusion makes popping noises as it exits the die and tears at the blowouts.

■ Trapped air is making the noise; air bubbles are breaking with force as the piece is extruded. *Wedge the clay better.*

Top: JENNIFER LAPHAM, *Nest,* 1996. 5 x 3 x 4 feet (150 x 90 x 120 cm). Stoneware; bisque-fired extruded tubes stacked, tied, and wrapped with wet slip and strips of fabric; cone 08.

Bottom: JENNIFER LAPHAM, *Presence and Absence,* 1996. 6 x 4 feet (180 x 120 cm) in room 10 x 10 x 10 feet (300 x 300 x 300 cm). Stoneware; bisque-fired, extruded tubes; cone 08. Photos by J.A. Lapham

TO CONSTRUCT YOUR FLIP PLATTER,
YOU WILL NEED:

APPROXIMATELY 20 LBS. (9.08 KG)
OF CLAY BODY (FOR BOTH PLATTER
AND EXTRUSIONS)

SHEETS OF NEWSPAPER

PLATTER PATTERN (OPTIONAL)

PLASTIC GARBAGE BAG OR SHEETS
OF PLASTIC

2 SQ. FT. (.18 M²) OF FOAM RUBBER

WOODEN ROLLING PIN

SMOOTH METAL RIB

2 WOOD BOARDS (A LITTLE BIGGER
THAN YOUR PLATTER DESIGN)

POTTER'S KNIFE

RULER OR TAPE MEASURE (OPTIONAL)

EXTRUDER

2 DIES: A TRAPEZOIDAL DIE FOR SUP-
PORT PIECES (FIG. 1), AND A DIE FOR
THE FOOT RING (FIG. 2)

2 LIGHTWEIGHT PLASTIC BATS

SMALL SURFORM TOOL WITH HANDLE

WOODEN TOOL WITH ONE SPOON-
SHAPED END

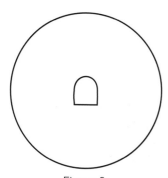

Figure 2

1 Start by rolling an even slab of clay approximately 16 x 16 inches (40 x 40 cm) and ⅜ inch (9 mm) thick. The slab's thickness depends on the size of the platter; if you choose to make a platter smaller than approximately 16 x 16 inches (40 x 40 cm), a ⅜-inch (9 mm) thickness will work fine. Larger platters will require a thicker slab. A thickness of ⁷⁄₁₆ to ½ inch (1.1 to 1.3 cm) will be enough for most larger platters. If your slab is too thick, the end result will be a platter that is too heavy to use comfortably.

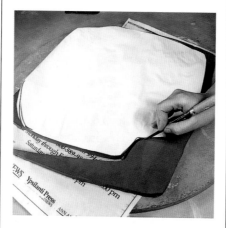

2 Using a smooth metal rib, refine both surfaces of the slab.

3 Lay a single sheet of newspaper on top of a board placed on your work surface, then position the slab on top. (The newspaper will keep the slab from sticking to the board.) Using the paper pattern you've designed as a guide or working freehand, cut the slab with a potter's knife to the desired shape for your platter.

4 Next, measure or eyeball the edges of your platter. Using the die you have designed, extrude enough pieces to fit along the platter's edge—three or four pieces totaling about 5 or 6 lineal feet (150 to 180 cm). These will support the rim and create the well of your platter.

5 Tear 3-inch-wide (7.5 cm) strips of newspaper and place them around the edge of the platter, so that the soft extrusions don't stick to the slab. On top of these strips, position the extrusions upside down along the platter's edge, aligning the extrusion's tall, outside face with the platter's outside edge. (Remember that the outside edge of the rim should be supported by the highest side of the trapezoid.) Cut and place the extrusions end to end, but do not physically join them. The less you handle the extrusions, the better they will keep their shape.

6 Cover the slab and extrusions with another single sheet of newspaper, then place another board on top of the whole construction— newspaper, extrusions, and slab.

7 Now you're ready to flip the platter. Sandwich the bottom and top boards between your hands, and flip the structure over in a quick, up-and-over motion. (If you are making a

very large platter, the structure may be a little unwieldy, and you may need some help.) Upward momentum will keep the extrusions in place as you flip the structure over. Remove the board that is now on top.

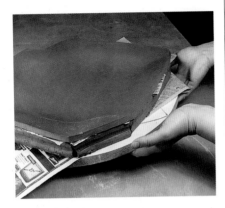

8 Carefully shake and tap the remaining bottom board. This will encourage the slab to fall into the center well formed by the extrusions.

9 You should now have a platter with rims sloping to a center well, formed by the extruded supports. Pull up gently on the outside edges of the extrusions so that they sit flat on the board beneath. If you want a more defined slope on the interior of the platter, use the palm of your hand to gently press the clay down into the center well.

10 Next, you'll need to extrude enough foot ring segments to follow the bottom contour of the platter, a few inches in from the edge. The foot ring's mass and dimensions must be appropriate to the mass and

dimensions of the platter; they can be more generous than the foot rings usually seen on industrial ware (industrial processes and machinery only allow minimal foot rings). *(Note: The flat side of the die shape in fig. 2 represents the side of the extrusion that will be attached to the bottom of the plate.)*

Do not join the ends of the foot segments just yet. Shape the segments to the approximate contour of the platter bottom, leaving extra length for cutting and joining. For now, store the segments in the well of the platter to stiffen. It is important that later, when they are joined and attached to the platter, they have the same stiffness as the platter.

11 Loosely wrap the platter in a single sheet of plastic and allow it to stiffen for a day or two until it is leather-hard. (If you choose, you can speed up the stiffening process by carefully using a heat lamp, heat gun, hair dryer, or fan, but make sure the platter is uniformly stiffened. The platter is ready for the next step when it holds its shape well but the clay has not changed color or begun to show other signs of drying.

12 When the platter is leather-hard, remove the stored foot ring segments and set them aside. Place several pieces of sheet foam rubber into the platter's center to a level approximately 2 inches (5 cm) above the rim (but not on the rim).

13 Completely remove the supporting extrusions from under the rim. The rim will not sag if the platter is stiff enough.

14 The next step is to flip the platter again. This time, place a plastic bat (lighter and smaller than the board) on top of the positioned foam rubber sheets; carefully flip the structure—including platter, foam, and bat—over, and place it on your work surface. The platter will now be upside down, balanced on the foam, with the rim suspended about 1 inch (2.5 cm) above the bat. The rim should not touch the bat, and no weight should be resting on the rim. *(Note: In this position, the rim is safe from stresses that might cause it to crack or flatten. If the platter warps out of shape in this position, it was not yet stiff enough to flip, and should be returned to its extruded supports.)*

If the platter holds its shape, it is ready for the addition of a foot ring, which usually parallels the platter's edge. For the foot ring to support the cantilever of the rim, it must be positioned just where the angle of the sides meets the bottom. If the distance from the foot ring to the outer edge is more than 4 inches (10 cm), the rim may fall during firing or crack from the edge toward the center.

15 To make the foot ring, you'll need to join the shaped segments that you made in step 10. Score and dampen the area where the ring will join the platter. Score the flat side of the foot ring segments and, one at a time, place and press them in position on the bottom, cutting, scoring, and joining ends as you proceed. Pull up gently to test the join.

16 Using the same method you used in steps 7 and 14, place a bat big enough to fully support the foot ring on top of the foot ring, and flip the structure—with bats, foam, and platter—again.

17 Remove the top bat and foam. The platter will be standing on its foot on the bottom bat, and is nearly complete.

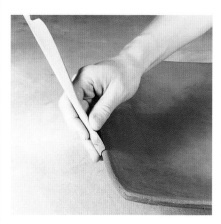

18 You will need to round and refine the edges of the platter for both aesthetic and functional reasons (to prevent chipping). Use a Surform plane to round off the edges and a wooden tool to polish them. You can quickly modify a wooden tool that will work especially well for this purpose. Use a round file to create and sharpen an arc-shaped dent in one end of a standard wooden tool, then draw the arc around the platter's edges to round and polish them. The platter is ready: A two-sided canvas on which to explore and enjoy painting or carving, pattern or imagery, and finally glaze color and sheen.

CHAPTER FIVE

EXTRUSION, MOLDMAKING, AND PRESS MOLDING

Diana Pancioli, *Platter*, 1990. 14 x 10 inches (35 x 25 cm). Stoneware; pressed from a mold made from an extruded model; reduction fired to cone 10.
Photo by artist. Collection of T. Dietrich.

As THE PREVIOUS CHAPTER shows, extrusion can be used with handbuilding to create beautiful, unique works in clay. It can also be used in combination with moldmaking and press molding to create multiples of an object. Once you're familiar with how these three processes work together, you can use them to efficiently produce multiples of utilitarian forms such as platters, trays, and bowls. The same freedom offered by "flip platter" design in the previous chapter holds true for creating ware with a combination of extrusion, moldmaking, and press molding.

Learning to use extrusion with moldmaking and press molding is more time consuming at first than, for example, learning the flip technique shown in chapter 4. Here you are learning three processes: making a model from extrusion, casting and finishing a plaster mold from the clay model, and finally, pressing and finishing the clay piece. Although there are more steps than for other methods, the steps themselves aren't difficult. And it's a worthwhile process to learn, as it offers a way to make multiples more easily than by using other methods.

There are other ways than those shown here to use extruded forms as models. Extruded forms, both solid and hollow, can provide the initial parts from which models are designed. Solid forms can be extruded, cut, and joined to invent forms that can serve as models for two-piece or multi-part molds for pressing or slip casting.

Molds, if carefully handled, last a long time—through many pressings. They can be used to create small and large sculptural and functional forms, from a few inches to a few feet in any dimension. Once made, molds can even change function, serving first to make a utilitarian object and later a sculptural segment, or the reverse.

CREATING A PLATTER USING AN EXTRUDED MOLD

The "flip platter" technique shows how to create a single platter. But if you want to make a series of platters, or plates identical in size and shape, using extrusion to make models and molds and pressing them is an efficient way to go about it. Press molding is ideal for platters, as cross-sectional thickness (and therefore weight) can be well controlled. The following information provides step-by-step instructions to create a medium-sized platter, with ideas for size and construction variations.

Top: ELINA BRANDT-HANSEN, *Fractal Star*, 1997. 4¾ x 24 x 2 inches (12 x 60 x 5 cm). Colored stoneware and white porcelain; extruded coils with some wrapped in porcelain.
Bottom: detail, *Fractal Star*. Photos by Rune Saevig.

DESIGNING A PLATTER FOR EXTRUSION, MOLDMAKING, AND PRESS MOLDING

Designing a platter using this combination of techniques is much the same as for the "flip" platter in chapter 4, with an added option: You can simply cut and arrange extrusions until you find a form you like; or you can cut a paper pattern as before, place it on a large formica-covered bat, and trace around the pattern with a permanent marker. The pattern should be smaller than the bat by about 3 inches all around.

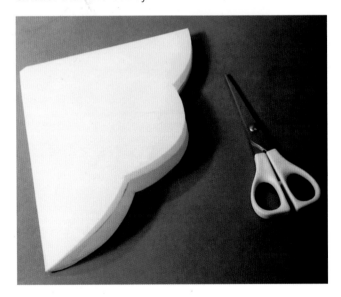

DIE DESIGN FOR SMALL, MEDIUM, AND LARGE PLATTERS

(Note: See fig. 1 for all die shapes referred to in this section, unless otherwise noted.)

You'll need two solid dies to create the extrusions from which you'll construct a medium-sized platter model. (Later, when you're pressing the plate, you'll also use a foot ring die—see fig. 2 in chapter 4.) One die (D) will form the platter's rim and well; the other die (C) will create the mold edge and dam.

If you are making a smaller platter (approximately 10 inches [25 cm] or less in diameter), one die (B) will form three parts of the plate—the rim, well, and mold edge. A second die (A) will create just the band which dams the plaster when pouring the mold.

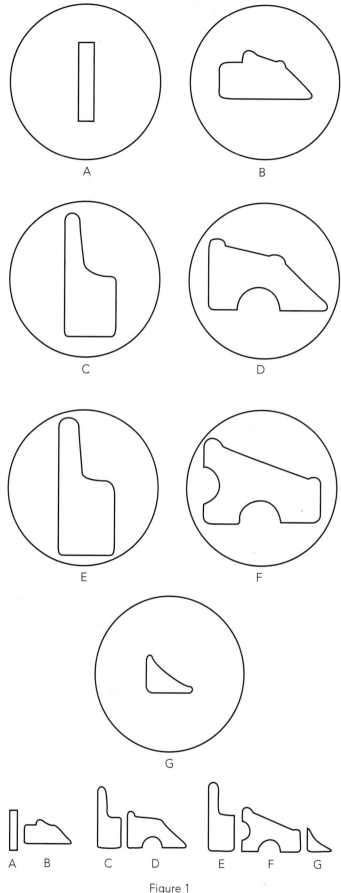

For a larger platter (18 or so inches [45 cm] wide or long), you will need three dies; and again each die will form different parts. The first die (G) will create the well of the platter (the inside slope); another (F) will form the rim; and a third (E) will create the dam and plate edge. (Note: The limitations of a 4-inch [10 cm] extruder mean that the larger the platter and its parts, the more the forming of parts must be divided among different dies. If you use a bigger extruder, it will be able to accommodate the making of larger platter parts, so you'll need fewer dies.)

As you create your dies, keep in mind that their design will determine many aspects of the finished platter's makeup—the angle of the rim's rise, the rim's width, the edge shape, and the depth of the platter. The angle of the platter's rim should be raised, not level; a horizontal rim may fall during firing. The rim may or may not have a thickened or "beaded" edge—a rounded protrusion along the edge of the rim, as on a molding, created by a drill bit larger than the rim's wall thickness. A good reason to make a rim with a raised bead is that after pressing the platter, when flashings left from pressing have to be trimmed away, a bead will clearly indicate the trimming line. Either way, the rim's edge should be rounded to protect against chipping.

The width of the platter's rim can be wide or narrow depending on your preference, but certain limitations help determine it. The size of your extruder's die holder will in part determine rim width. A medium-sized platter, like the one for which instructions are provided below, cannot support a rim that extends much more than 3 inches (7.5 cm) beyond its foot—another limitation. The platter's thickness will also determine how far the platter rim can extend without warping, cracking, or falling during firing.

Figure 1

PHASE ONE: MAKING A MODEL FOR THE MOLD

THE FIRST STEP IN CONSTRUCTING YOUR PLATTER IS TO MAKE A MODEL FOR THE MOLD. TO DO THIS, YOU'LL NEED:

PLATTER PATTERN (OPTIONAL)

APPROXIMATELY 25 LBS. (11.35 KG) OF CLAY BODY

2 DIES (D AND C IN FIG. 1)

LARGE FORMICA-COVERED BAT OR BOARD, APPROXIMATELY 18 INCHES (45 CM) IN DIAMETER

POTTER'S KNIFE, CHEESE WIRE, OR TOGGLE WIRE

WOODEN TOOL WITH ONE SPOON-SHAPED END

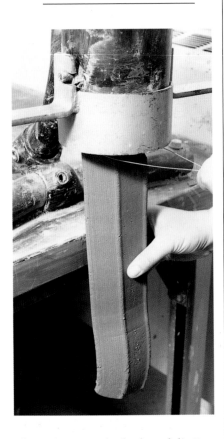

1 Using your clay body and die D, extrude enough pieces to fit around your pattern, with some length to spare. These sections will comprise the platter's rim and well.

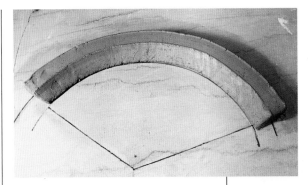

2 Next, cut and position these extrusions around the pattern. This process will vary depending on your platter's design. If the design is curved, bend the extrusions to shape as soon as they are extruded. Curves can be difficult to bend if they are sharp, but most curves can be accomplished by gentle shaping or by cutting and joining sections. If the design includes straight lines or sharp angles, you may need to bevel-cut the extrusions, which often wastes a few inches on each end. If bevels are necessary, pull longer extrusions.

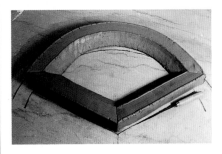

To avoid distorting the extrusion ends when you cut them, use a sharp potter's knife, cheese wire, or toggle wire. Cut and re-cut them until they fit closely against the end of the next extrusion. When you place the extrusions along the pattern, don't worry about tiny gaps between extrusions; you needn't fill them or attempt to smooth transitions. The less you touch the extrusions (other than cutting them), the more regular your mold will be. Small gaps will become thin plaster "flashings," little protrusions of plaster that can easily be trimmed off later. (Gaps create

"outies," which are best corrected after the plaster is set.) At this stage, only "innies"—irregularities that protrude from the model and will cast as holes in the mold—need to be smoothed.

Once the extrusions are in place, the construction will look very much like the platter you will later take from the mold—its rim and well shaped by the extrusions, its floor shaped by the formica bat. The rim and well extrusion may not make a smooth transition with the bat, but this will be best corrected later, after the mold is made. (Critique your platter form at this point and make any changes you wish. Consider the proportion of rim width to the size of the platter, and the depth in relation to width.)

3 Now, using die C, extrude sections that will be placed around the outside of the already positioned extrusions, to form both the rim and mold edges, and the dam. When you place the second extrusion against the first, you will see that the inner part of the second joins at ⅜ inch (9 mm) below the first. The depression, created by placing the second, shorter extrusion against the first, will fill with plaster and create the outer edge of the platter rim and the mold's edge. You want your mold to extend beyond the rim by about an inch (2.5 cm). The thickness of the platter at its rim will be ⅜ inch (9 mm).

The outer part of the same extrusion will form a dam to hold poured plaster in place. The dam section will be taller than the rim by about 1½ inches (3.8 cm); its height determines the thickness of the plaster mold at its outer edge. Molds need to be thick enough to be sturdy and absorbent, but not so thick that they are excessively heavy. You will carry your molds as well as flip them over in your hands; your wrists will suffer if the molds are heavier than they need to be.

4 Place these extruded dam sections closely around the outside of the already positioned extrusions. To prevent leaks when the plaster is poured, seal all vertical seams with clay on the outside, and place and press a pencil-thick coil of clay along the extrusion's outside base.

5 Once all the extrusions are in place, leave them uncovered for an hour to firm up enough to hold in the wet plaster. Extrusions that are too soft may collapse when the plaster is poured, but over-drying will make them shrink, creating gaps through which plaster will leak.

VARIATION

Making a platter of a different shape, in this case a rectangle, requires the same first steps as for the fan-shaped platter project—drawing the shape on a

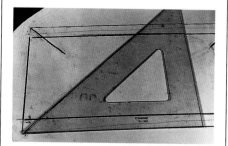

Design a rectilinear platter, and with a marker draw its shape onto a smooth surface. Use a plastic square to plan bevel cuts at corners.

Use platter dies C and D (or A and B, depending on the size platter you want) to extrude pieces for the platter's outline. Wire-cut bevels and place the extrusions on the drawing

Critique the platter's form and prepare the model for pouring.

This pressed and footed platter was made from the rectilinear mold.

smooth surface, extruding sections with dies C and D, then cutting the extrusions to fit and placing them on the drawing.

PHASE TWO: POURING THE MOLD

ONCE YOU HAVE A MODEL FOR THE MOLD, YOU'RE READY TO POUR THE MOLD. FOR THIS PHASE OF THE PROJECT, YOU'LL NEED:

NON-STICK VEGETABLE SPRAY

20 LBS. (9.08 KG) OF POTTERY PLASTER

SCOOP OR CAN FOR ADDING PLASTER

PLASTIC MIXING BOWL

YOUR CLAY MODEL

SOFT NYLON SCRUB PAD

SURFORM TOOL

A FEW SHARP LOOP TOOLS

WET/DRY SANDPAPER (OPTIONAL)

FAN (OPTIONAL)

CLOSE PROXIMITY TO A SINK AND WATER

1 Start by making a final check on your model to ensure that it is ready to hold plaster. Reinforce where necessary any vertical seams, and make sure that the clay dam is sufficiently stiff and that its bottom outside edges are properly sealed. Next, lightly coat the bat's formica surface, which will form the inside bottom of the platter, with a green soap, non-stick vegetable spray, or other releasing agent. Go easy applying the releasing agent you choose—the mold's surface must be porous, and too much releasing agent can diminish its porosity. Do not coat the clay extrusions; it's not necessary, and touching them may distort them.

An inexpensive 4-quart (3.8 L) plastic bowl will work well for mixing the plaster for your platter mold. The plaster you buy may be accompanied by the manufacturer's plaster/water ratio table; if not, basic steps for mixing plaster are simple. Fill the bowl just less than half full with cold water—hot water will cause the plaster to set more quickly. Add the plaster at a moderate pace, shaking it gently from a scoop or can all over the surface of the water, not sprinkling or dumping it. You'll know the mix is nearing correct proportions when the plaster stops sinking into the water and begins to make low mounds on the surface. Don't allow unabsorbed plaster to make high mounds.

With one hand, reach below the mixture's surface and squeeze out any lumps, then stir the mixture with your hand still below the surface. This will reduce the number of air bubbles that form.

After two or three minutes of stirring, when the mixed plaster feels just slightly thickened, it's ready to be poured. (Note: The total time elapsed for squeezing lumps and stirring should not exceed four minutes, or the plaster may begin to set.) The plaster should be neither too watery nor too thick. Watery plaster puts more pressure on the clay dam, and can cause the dam to break and the plaster to leak, and plaster that is too thick will not flow and fill the details of the mold.

3 Pour the plaster slowly and steadily into the center of the clay model. It will climb up the sides, fill in the recesses in the extrusions, and distribute itself levelly. If it doesn't level naturally, use your hand to move the plaster toward the construction's edges. Some mold makers use a soft brush early in the first pour, while the plaster is still fluid, to brush plaster into details and remove bubbles. Fill the mold with plaster to the level of the dam. When the first pour is complete, gently pound your work surface with your fist a few times. This will settle the plaster into the mold and allow small bubbles to rise to the surface.

If your first batch of plaster doesn't fill the mold, immediately estimate the amount you'll need to finish filling it, use a clean container to mix a second batch, and pour it as soon as possible. (The first layer will still be soft, or just beginning to set.) Do not move the mold for an hour or so. Plaster undergoes chemical changes, generating heat, as it sets. The mold should not be moved until the plaster has begun to cool.

2 Now you're ready to mix plaster which, poured and set, will become your mold. Figuring out how much plaster to mix for a particular mold gets easier with experience—you'll learn to eyeball the right amount. Until then, it's better to mix too little than too much. A mold doesn't have to be poured all at once. It can be poured in two layers, and you can mix more as you need it. For the mold that will make the platter in this project, you'll need 5 to 10 lbs. (2.27 to 4.54 kg.).

remove protrusions that could chip off into the eventual pressed platter. Basically, you're just cleaning up the mold. But do it carefully—you can't put back what you carve away.

Using a Surform tool, plane off sharp edges on both the bottom and top of the mold. Remove any undercuts that might prevent the mold from releasing the clay platter. Redefine the curve where the well meets the bottom of the platter, and refine other areas—grooves and joins—with sharp loop tools.

4 The next steps are to remove the clay rim and dam extrusions, and refine the mold, which can be done either when the mold is still warm or has cooled. If you choose to begin work on the mold when it's still warm, be careful. Working with the plaster at this stage, when it is still soft, has advantages and disadvantages. It can be carved—but also breaks—more easily. You may prefer to wait until the mold feels cool to the touch and the plaster is hard to remove the dam and rim extrusions and release the mold from its form.

Once the extrusions are removed, you may discover that despite using a releasing agent, the mold is stuck to the bat. If this happens, hold the bat and mold at a slight angle to the floor and tap the bat's edge very gently against the floor. Be careful. Make sure you hold on to the mold while tapping, as the mold may release suddenly, sliding down the bat and crashing to the floor.

5 In refining and finishing the mold, you'll want to remove unintentional flashings and other irregularities that result from the mold making process. Some of these are caused by "innies" allowed to remain during mold making. You should also

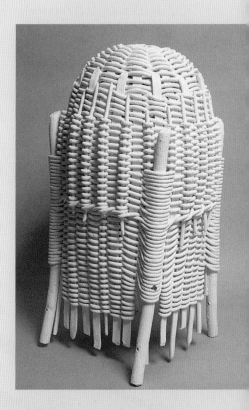

Top: **LAURIE ROLLAND**, *Sacarum for a Vessel*, 1997. 18 x 11 x 4½ inches (45 x 28 x 12 cm). Stoneware; assembled textured slabs and slabs made from extruded straps, thrown vessel; cone 6. Photo by artist.

Bottom: **RINA PELEG**, *White Porcelain #2*, 1985. 35 x 20 x 20 inches (87.5 x 50 x 50 cm). White clay; extruded coils; cone 04. Photo by artist.

6 When the mold is as you want it, you're ready for the final finishing step. In a sink, wash the mold in cold water, gently rubbing its surface with a soft nylon pad. This will remove most remaining surface bumps and imperfections. Don't scrub too hard—you may remove important details with overly vigorous rubbing. The mold will

now be clean, smooth, and very wet. If you want a super smooth surface, you can use wet/dry sandpaper of increasingly fine grit to sand your mold.

Otherwise, give it a once over, checking the form and surface. Make any necessary changes, then prop it up at an angle in front of a slow fan for a day, or let it dry naturally. Don't dry it with heat.

PHASE THREE: PRESS MOLDING THE PLATTER

WHEN YOUR MOLD IS COMPLETELY DRY, YOU'RE READY TO PRESS MOLD THE PLATTER. YOU'LL NEED:

10 LBS. (4.54 KG) OF CLAY BODY

PLASTIC GARBAGE BAG OR SHEETS OF PLASTIC

1 SHEET OF HEAVY-DUTY DRAWING PAPER (OPTIONAL)

CLEAR SELF-STICKING VINYL SHEETS (OPTIONAL)

ROLLING PIN

SLAB ROLLER (OPTIONAL)

FOOT RING DIE (CHAPTER 4, FIG. 2)

METAL RIBS, SMOOTH AND SERRATED

SPONGE OR SAND-FILLED SOCK (OPTIONAL)

HARD RUBBER RIB

SURFORM TOOL

BANDING WHEEL OR TURNTABLE (OPTIONAL)

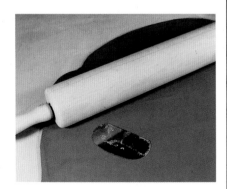

1 Use a rolling pin (or slab roller) to roll a ⅜-inch (9 mm) slab of clay to a size approximately 3 inches

(7.5 cm) larger all around than the mold you've created. This slab will form the entire platter. If you are making a platter smaller or larger than the one described in the preceding instructions, you'll need to roll a thinner or thicker slab, accordingly. Slab thickness depends on the size of the mold you are working with, the type of clay you are using, and, to some degree, your personal preferences. *(Note: If you use a slab roller, be sure to turn the slab over and roll it again with a rolling pin, to eliminate warping tendencies the slab roller may cause.)*

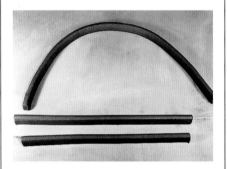

2 Next, using your foot ring die, extrude enough length plus a little extra to form the platter's foot ring. Lay the extrusions on a board in the approximate shape of the bottom of the platter, then set them aside covered loosely with a plastic sheet. The foot ring will stiffen slightly while you are pressing the platter. Further on in the process, when you join the slab and foot ring, their stiffnesses must be similar to avoid differences in shrinkage that can cause cracking.

3 Now you're ready to cut the slab, which should be approximately 3 inches (7.5 cm) larger all around than the mold. The difference is necessary because the mold has depth and the flat slab must accommodate that depth. Be careful, though—a slab that is too large will be more difficult to lift and place on the mold.

You can just eyeball and cut, or, if you plan to use the mold often, make a template to use as a guide for cutting. A template can be cut from heavy paper and laminated with shelf-liner plastic to waterproof it.

4 Using a metal rib, smooth both the top and bottom of the cut slab. Pick up the smoothed slab with flat hands (palms and fingers extended in the same plane and directly opposite each other on opposite sides of the slab). Place one edge of the slab at one edge of the mold and lower the slab onto the mold, as if you were closing a book cover. The slab should be centered on the mold, overlapping the edges.

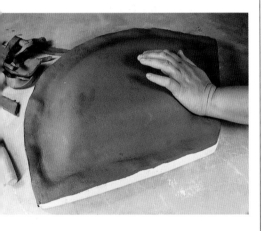

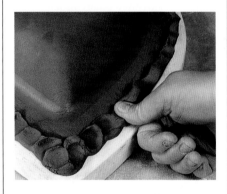

5 Reach over the mold and, with both hands, pull the edge of the clay slab toward you without folding it. Put inward pressure on the edge of the slab, to make it conform to the sides of the platter. Turn the platter slowly and repeat this motion all around it.

6 Using the palms of your hands, press the slab gently onto the mold and coax it to take the mold's shape. You can also use a small wrung-out sponge, or a sand-filled sock, to cozy the clay up against the platter's side walls. Running your finger around the platter where the sides meet the rim will allow you to detect any pockets of space remaining between the slab and mold. The aim is to press the slab tightly to the mold without thinning or denting the slab. It takes a little practice, but is very easy after a few tries. Now trim the slab to the edge of the mold, being careful to not trim plaster into your scrap clay.

7 Next, using both hands, bend a section of the slab's edge up with your fingers and stuff it gently down and into the outside edge of the rim (or into the bead if there is one). Repeat this process all around the rim.

When the edge is standing up all around the rim and positioned in the rim edge (or bead), push the clay straight down into the rim a thumb-width at a time. (Pushing straight down will not allow air to be folded into the rim.) Don't delay in completing these steps, because the clay must still be soft to properly take the mold's form.

8 When the slab edge is thumbed into the rim bead, thumb it all around once more to be sure it is well pressed. Then, using a hard rubber rib, smooth the thumbed area all around the platter. Only work the rim. Do not disturb the areas next to the rim (the platter's well and sides).

9 When you are satisfied that the rim is compressed, remove excess clay with a Surform tool angled toward the rim edge. Remember, the rim is not horizontal but rises at an angle. Next, you can smooth the underside of the rim with a rubber or metal rib, getting rid of marks left by the Surform. This is your last chance to refine the underside of the rim. Once the platter is off the mold, you will apply as little pressure as possible to the rim, as pressure can cause warping or cracking. (Do not yet remove the platter from the mold.)

PHASE FOUR: ATTACHING THE FOOT RING

NOW YOU'RE READY TO ATTACH THE PLATTER'S FOOT-RING. TO DO THIS, YOU WILL NEED:

THE FOOT RING SECTIONS YOU EXTRUDED AND SET ASIDE IN STEP 2 OF PHASE 3

POTTER'S KNIFE

CHEESE WIRE

WOODEN TOOL

SERRATED METAL RIB

1 The foot ring's placement will vary depending on the shape of your platter. (Press molding the same platter many times will give you the opportunity to try the foot ring in different locations, to find the placement that is structurally and visually optimal.) For maximum structural support, the foot ring should be placed at the point where the platter's sides meet its bottom, echoing the platter's outside edge. The foot ring supports the cantilever of the rim; if the distance between foot ring and rim edge exceeds 3 or 4 inches (7.5 or 10 cm), the rim may fall or crack from edge to center during firing. Proper placement will help support an extended rim.

If the foot ring is placed too far under the bottom of the piece, it will push an unsightly ridge up into the bottom of the platter, and the rim may sag or crack. A foot placed too far from the center may allow the glazed bottom to touch the kiln shelf during firing; a foot that's tall enough and correctly placed will give adequate clearance.

2 To determine the foot ring's position on the bottom of the platter, hold your hand over the rim with your index finger along the outside edge of the mold and your thumb on the bottom of the platter. Moving your hand stiffly (like a "jig"), keeping the distance between index finger and thumb the same, score a line with your thumbnail all around the platter where the platter's sides meet the bottom. This method will help you determine placement of a foot ring even on an irregularly shaped platter. (You can also use a banding wheel, if you have one, to ease this step.)

3 Score and dampen the foot ring segments and a ¾-inch-wide (1.9 cm) band on the bottom of the platter indicated by your thumb mark. Join the foot ring sections end to end as you go (not all at once) by miter-cutting the ends of adjacent pieces, scoring and pressing them together. Press the sections firmly onto the bottom of the platter, and pull up on them gently to test the joins. When the foot ring is attached, polish it with a knife or a wooden tool. Allow the clay construction to dry for about an hour, until the foot ring and platter are stiff.

PHASE FIVE: FINISHING THE PLATTER

THE LAST STEPS IN COMPLETING THE PROJECT ARE TO REMOVE THE PLATTER FROM THE MOLD AND REFINE IT BEFORE SLIPPING, CARVING, OR DRYING IT IN PREPARATION FOR GLAZING AND FIRING. YOU'LL NEED:

PLASTIC BAT (OPTIONAL)

SURFORM TOOL

WOODEN TOOL

1 Test the platter's readiness by gently lifting up on its edges. If the platter seems to be loose, place a plastic bat on it that is just large enough to completely cover the foot ring. Place one hand on the bat and the other hand under the mold, and flip the whole structure over. The platter will be standing on its foot, with the weight of the mold on it. Quickly and carefully lift the mold from the platter. If the mold does not release the platter, turn it back over and let the platter dry a while longer.

2 When the mold is removed and the platter is standing on its foot ring, you'll be able to see how well you pressed the form. The final step is to clean up the edges. A Surform tool works well to trim away any rim flashings back to the rim's true molded edge. A wooden tool or plastic credit card cut with an indented arc at one end will nicely polish the edge. When construction is complete, another platter can be started on the same mold while the first platter is slipped, carved, or dried, to be biscuit fired, glazed, and fired.

VARIATION

A found form such as an oval metal tray can be enhanced with extrusion and then molded to make beautiful functional ware. Although trays are too flat to use as molds directly, they can, with extruded edges added, become great platters for press molding. The following steps and photos show the process of using an extrusion-enhanced found form to make a mold. If you opt to use this technique, you'll need to refer to corresponding phases in the Medium-Sized Platter project, above, for materials, tools, and steps not detailed below.

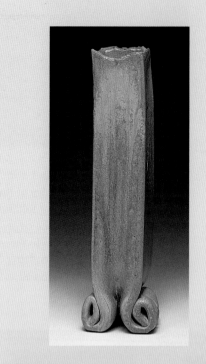

Top: GINNY MARSH, *Vase*, 1997. 11¼ x 3¼ x 2¼ inches (28.13 x 8.13 x 5.63 cm). Protoporcelain; extruded, with bottom portion cut and rolled; cone 10.

Bottom: John Troup, *Extruded Vases*, 1999. From left to right: 3 x 3 x 12 inches (7.5 x 7.5 x 30 cm); 4½ x 4½ x 20 inches (11.25 x 11.25 x 50 cm); 8 x 8 x 32 inches (20 x 20 x 80 cm). Stoneware; hollow extrusion torqued as extruded; cone 10. Photo by artist.

The platters shown at top and center were made using an extrusion-enhanced form. Pictured at bottom is the back side of the platter shown immediately above it.

MOLD FROM AN EXTRUSION-ENHANCED FOUND FORM

1 Extrude a decorative or beaded band and lay it on the rim of the tray.

2 Without distorting the extrusion, bend, wire-cut, and fit the band to the rim. There is no need to score and join—just lay the extrusion in place.

3 Use die C (see fig. 1) to create extrusions for the mold's rim and dam, and place these around the tray. You may have to cut the extrusions to adjust their heights so that they are equivalent with the tray's height.

4 Pour, finish, and dry the mold.

7 Work the underside of the rim with a Surform tool.

10 Finish the seam, invert the plate, and remove the mold.

5 Roll a ⅜-inch (9 mm) slab of clay to a size 3 or so inches (7.5 cm) larger all around than the mold, then cut the slab to a size and shape 3 inches (7.5 cm) larger than the mold and echoing its shape. (At this point, you can also vary the platter by texturing the slab before pressing it onto the mold.)

8 Score the bottom of the plate.

11 Use a Surform tool to finish the platter's edge, then further refine it with a homemade wood or plastic edge tool.

9 Attach the foot ring.

6 Press the plate onto the mold.

CHAPTER SIX

EXTRUDED COMPONENTS

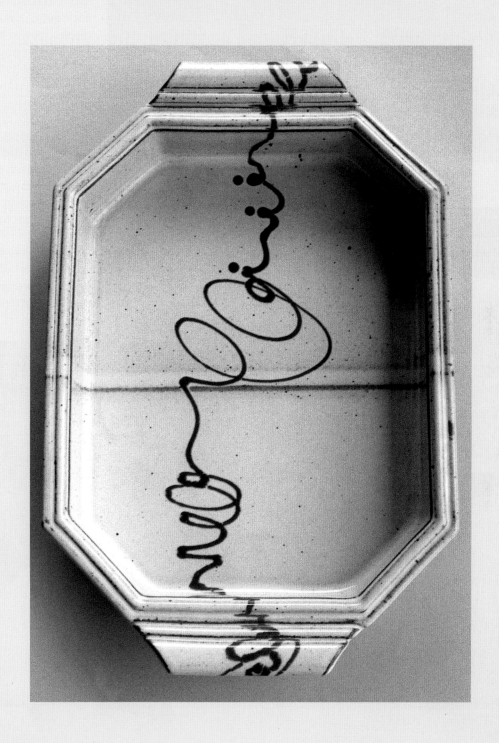

TY LARSEN, *Untitled,* 1982.
14 x 10 x 3 inches. (35 x 7.5 cm).
Stoneware; extruded and assembled with slab bottom; cone 10 reduction. Photo by Diana Pancioli.

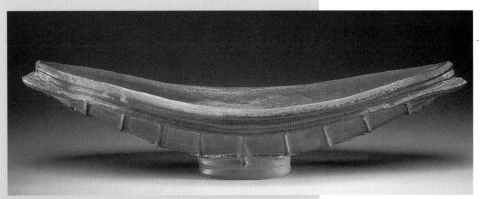

USED IN COMBINATION with other clay-working techniques such as slab building, press molding, and throwing, extruded clay forms can serve as the walls and feet of casseroles, dishes, bowls, planters, cups, and many other utilitarian items.

In this chapter, you'll learn how to make an oval, flat-bottomed dish and a variation of it—a bowl with a press molded, curved bottom. Step-by-step instructions and photos show you how to construct an oval container that can be modified to become a baking dish, serving dish, or planter. The following pages also offer information and examples of variations of this form, including higher- and lower-walled containers, textured walls, press molded and thrown bottoms, and the additions of rims, handles, feet, galleries, and lids.

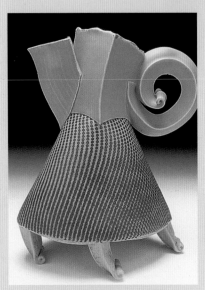

Top: RANDY JOHNSTON, *Long Boat Form*, 1999. 28 x 7 inches (70 x 17.5 cm). Stoneware with fluxed kaolin slip; extruded, altered, and assembled; wood-fired to cone 10. Photo by Peter Lee.

Center: D. HAYNE BAYLESS, *Square Teapot with Hinged Lid*, 10 x 12 x 7 inches (25 x 30 x 17.5 cm). Stoneware; extruded spout, hinge, handle, and legs; cone 10 reduction.

Bottom: D. HAYNE BAYLESS, *Pitcher*, 12 x 10 x 6 inches (30 x 25 x 15 cm). Stoneware; slab body with extruded spout, neck, handle, and feet; cone 10 reduction.

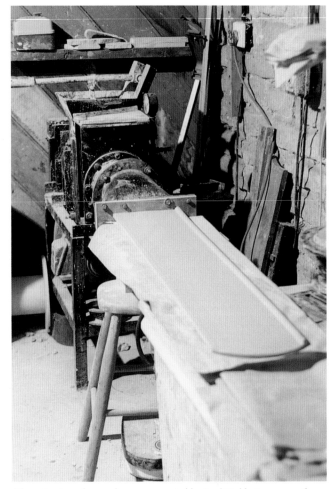

The extrusions shown above were created by Paul Stubbs to serve as the walls of large planters.

Paul Stubbs assembling the extruded walls of a planter.

EXTRUDED WALLS

Forming walls with extrusion is both efficient and creative—objects can be made with speed and easy variation. An extruded wall ribbon can create containers of infinitely varied shapes. In addition to round and oval shapes, it can create forms that are rectilinear,

Paul Stubbs makes wonderful wood-fired, salted planters like those pictured above using 3-foot stiffened sections of de-aired clay extruded with his homemade extruder. The pieces shown were made with a combination of Ball clay and Molochite, with the sides of each piece cut to a compound angle on a special cutter Stubbs designed and built.

Top: I.B. REMSEN, *Jewel Box*, 1979. 8 x 5 inches. Stoneware; extruded and assembled with additional slabs, decorated with raw slips, glazes, and overglaze oxides; cone 10 reduction.

Bottom: I.B. REMSEN, *Sunken Treasures Box*, 1979. 10 x 6 inches. Stoneware; extruded and assembled with additional slabs, decorated with raw slips, glazes, and overglaze oxides; cone 10 reduction. Photos by artist.

triangular, fan-shaped, lobed, organic, or geometric. You can use a wall extrusion in a long, continuous way, joining it at only one point to enclose a shape; or, to create forms with harder-edged angles and curves, you can cut the extrusion into pieces, making curved or straight sections joined in many places. In other words, when bevel-cut and joined, extrusions will produce sharp corners; when curved, cut, and pieced, they will create lobes.

To create the open box pictured at top right, David Hendley extruded the four sides in one 4-foot-long (120 cm) piece, then placed the extrusion on a newspaper-covered board to firm up. Using a single long extrusion to create all four sides of the box means that the slip design remains uninterrupted as it turns the corners of the box. Extrusions for two different boxes, as well as the die used, are pictured above. The die is made of black safety glass backed with ¾-inch (1.88 cm) plywood.

When dried to soft leather-hard stage, the sides of the box are cut to size with a piece of fishing line. For a four-sided box, each piece is cut at a 45-degree angle, using a miter box as a guide.

A wall section is essentially a flat ribbon of clay. The advantages of an extruded wall over a slab-cut wall are that it is dependably even in cross-section, and has edge shape and thickness designed in advance for your purpose. Extruded walls can incorporate useful or decorative thickenings ("beads") wherever needed, at upper or lower edges or elswhere. Extruded wall height (short, medium, or tall) can also

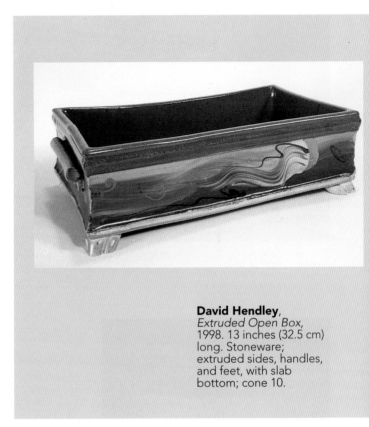

David Hendley, *Extruded Open Box*, 1998. 13 inches (32.5 cm) long. Stoneware; extruded sides, handles, and feet, with slab bottom; cone 10.

be designed to suit your purpose and is limited only by the diameter of your extruder barrel. Extruded walls can be joined to flat or shaped slab bottoms, press molded curved bottoms, or other shaped or textured bottoms.

Once you have learned to join a wall to a bottom, join extrusion ends, and seal a seam, you can create a container in any shape you desire, in a variety of sizes. Better still, relative to other clay processes, you can create them efficiently and quickly. Functional objects made with extruded walls are thin and light, and can be made without a high level of skill.

CREATING A DISH WITH EXTRUDED WALLS

Making a small, flat-bottomed dish is a good way to learn how to use extrusions as walls. The assortment of simple round and oval dishes in photo 1 were created from extrusions pulled in just a few minutes. The process is straightforward, relatively fast, and delivers a durable, attractive dish that can be used for whatever purpose appeals to you. One of the pleasures of working with extrusion is the ease of variation and correction it affords. It encourages a critical eye and adds spontaneity and interest to production work. This project began with the aim of making multiples of

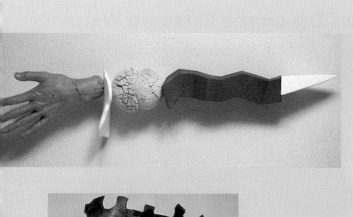

Top: TOM VENNER, *Reaching Back*, 1993. 18 x 4½ inches (45 x 11.25 cm). Mixed clays; extruded, press molded, and handbuilt; cone 06.
Center: FRANK STELLA AND FRANK BOSCO, *Jump Her Juberju*, 1985. 21 x 12 x 7 inches (52.5 x 30 x 17.5 cm).
Bottom: FRANK STELLA AND FRANK BOSCO, *The Plains of Baltimore*, 1985. 24 x 37 x 15 inches (60 x 92.5 x 37.5 cm).
Both Stella/Bosco pieces of shoe polish on cast steel; forms made in extruded terra-cotta by Bosco, with each form then cast by Stella in wax, then steel, then stainless steel, and assembled in composition. Photos by Allen Cohen.

Photo 1

one large oval dish, but the different lengths extruded that day, once curled on the table in preparation, inspired instead an assortment of variously shaped small- and medium-sized dishes .

DESIGNING A DISH WITH EXTRUDED WALLS

You can decide in advance what shape you'd like your dish to be, or you can let the design work happen organically, as you build. You can eyeball oval or round forms, or make templates for these shapes. For rectangular or square forms, you can use paper boxes as a guide for shaping. (Tissue boxes are nicely proportioned and readily available.) For example, you can cut the upper edge of a tissue box to a height ½ inch (1.3 cm) below the top (beaded) edge of the extrusion. Place a soft extrusion inside or outside the box, letting the box shape the corners, but do not join the extrusions. Use the dimensions of the bottom of the box plus an inch (2.5 cm) as a pattern to cut an approximate slab for the bottom. (Remove the box form as soon as the wall has stiffened slightly, after about half an hour.)

DIE DESIGN FOR EXTRUDED WALLS

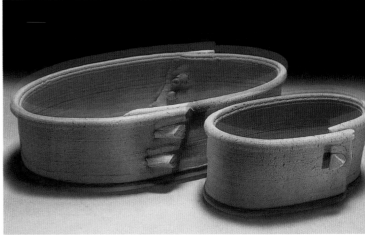

Photo 1

A single die will create extrusions to form the walls of a baking dish. The die shown in figure 2, a straight band with a rounded bead on one side, was used to create the dishes in photo 1. The dies shown in figure 1 and figure. 3 through 7 are shorter, longer, beaded, and curved varations. Fig. 8 shows a wall die with a gallery (the form that supports the lid) attached. The die shown in figure 9, a zigzag, was used to create the project in this chapter, but you can choose any wall die you like.

When you make your die for wall extrusions, bear in mind that an extrusion with a thickening (or rounded "bead") along the top edge will give the dish a more finished look and prevent against chipping. Wall extrusions can be designed with any number of beads anywhere you like—at the top, bottom, or between the two. While the top edge of your die should be rounded, the bottom should be flattened to join easily to a slab bottom. You can also design a slight thickening at the inside bottom of the die to add a little extra clay at the seam (instead of adding a coil later).

The thickness of the die wall you design will make your work lighter or heavier, and easier or more difficult to work with. A die wall that's too thin will make the extrusion hard to work with; if it's too thick, the object will be heavy. It will take a little experience to get the die thickness just the way you want it.

Oven heat also plays a part in determining die wall thickness. If you plan to make dishes to be used for baking, it's best to maintain a relatively even thickness in cross section for both walls and bottom—their thicknesses should be the same all over. The finished ware must heat evenly, or variations in thermal expansion may induce cracking.

Top: AYUMI HORI, *Porcelain Dish*, 1998. 3 x 6 x 6 inches (7.5 x 15 x 15 cm).

Top and bottom: Ayumi Hori's serving dishes are fine examples of the interesting variations in shape that are possible when using bands to construct walls. Although she threw the bands for these dishes on the wheel, they could have easily have been extruded.
Photos by Diana Pancioli.

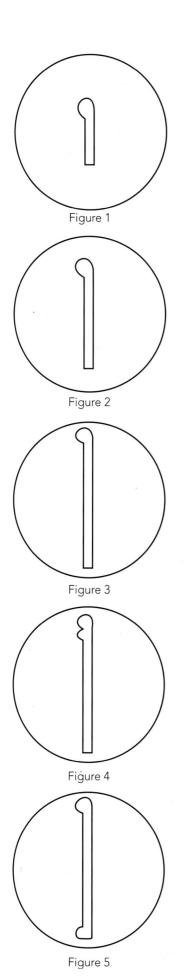

Figure 1

Figure 2

Figure 3

Figure 4

Figure 5

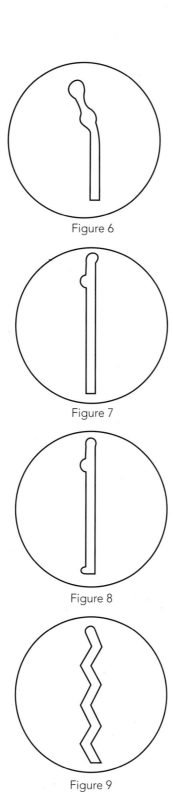

Figure 6

Figure 7

Figure 8

Figure 9

PROJECT
AN OVAL DISH

TO MAKE AN OVAL DISH LIKE THOSE SHOWN IN PHOTO 1, YOU'LL NEED:

10 TO 25 LBS. (4.54 TO 11.35 KG) OF YOUR CLAY BODY

A WALL DIE (FIGS. 1 THROUGH 7)

A LENGTH OF STRING LONGER THAN THE DIAMETER OF YOUR DISH DESIGN (OPTIONAL)

PLASTIC GARBAGE BAG OR SHEETS OF PLASTIC

WOODEN ROLLING PIN

EXTRUDER

SERRATED METAL RIB

MEDIUM-SIZED SOFT BRUSH

POTTER'S KNIFE

A WOODEN TOOL WITH ONE SPOON-SHAPED END

1 Before pulling any extrusions, you'll need to roll a slab to serve as the bottom of the dish—the slab needs a little time to stiffen. The slab should be larger than the dish you plan to make by a few inches all around. A ⅜-inch (9 mm) thickness is typically quoted for handbuilt ware, but I prefer ¼-inch (6 mm) thickness for small- and medium-sized items of 10-inch (25 cm) diameters or less. A larger dish (18 inches [45 cm] or more in diameter, width, or length) might need a little extra thickness—perhaps ½ inch (1.3 cm) or so. Within this ¼- to ½-inch (6 mm to 1.3 cm) range, determining thickness will be in part a judgment based on the size of the dish and your aesthetic preference. For larger items, you may also want a thicker wall die.

2 Using your wall die, extrude enough length to make the wall in one piece, plus a few extra inches. (This will depend on the size of the dish you're making.) You can visually estimate the length, or actually measure it. (A marked piece of string can serve as a rough guide for a rounded object's extruded length.) A full extruder barrel will yield more length than you need to make just one baking dish. If you wish, roll enough slabs to make a series of dishes, extrude the entire barrel of clay, and create a number of dishes all at once.

One extruded section will create the wall of the dish. Curl and place the soft extrusion, with its top (or beaded) edge down, on your work surface, and allow it to stiffen slightly—15 minutes to half an hour depending on the weather. The slab and the extrusion should be the same stiffness for the next step. (Curl extrusions only for rounded forms; leave them straight for rectilinear forms.)

3 Place the curled, stiffened wall section (still upside down) on top of the slab you've rolled, in the shape you've chosen for your dish. Do not press the sections onto the slab just yet. Cut the slab close around the perimeter of the wall, about ¼ inch (6 mm) away from the wall and at a 45° angle undercut. Remove the clay you've cut away from around the slab. Lift the extrusion off the slab and place it, still upside down, on your work surface. Use a serrated metal rib to score the bottom edge of the extrusion and the edge of the slab. Dampen the scored areas with a wet brush.

4 Carefully lift the extrusion, and this time place it right side up ⅛ inch (3 mm) inside the edge of the cut slab. At this point, just before you press the walls onto the bottom, you'll need to join the extrusion ends. There are a number of ways the extruded section's ends can be joined. Bevel-cutting will join them seamlessly end to end—score, join, and smooth the seam using your knife or a wooden tool. Or you can cut or tear and overlap them at the join.

Joins present an opportunity to interject personal style into your work—they can be smooth, rough, or ragged. Joins can be smoothed and hidden, left "fresh" and allowed to show, or you can borrow techniques used with other materials. You can lap joins to give the effect of an antique cheese box, or peg them as a woodworker might. The join can be riveted, laced, buttoned, or spliced.

5 Once the extrusion ends are joined, press the wall firmly onto the slab. Test the attachment by pulling up gently on the wall. To further strengthen the wall/bottom join,

run a spoon-shaped wooden tool around the outside of the dish under the edge of the slab. Use the tool with the roundness facing up to force the clay upward and into the join. You can run your finger around the seam to finish it or, after working on the inside seam, you can invert the dish, plane off the excess with a Surform tool, and smooth it with a wooden tool. (Plane just a little or you will thin and weaken the join.)

To finish and seal the inside seam, run the same rounded tool along the inside bottom edge. There is no need to add a coil to the inside seam. Adding soft coils to stiffened seams is time consuming and increases the risk of cracking at the seam due to shrinkage differences. At this point, you can add handles, if desired, or slip color.

6 Dry your dish under plastic for a day. When it is thoroughly dry, biscuit fire it, then glaze it and fire it again. If you are making a dish to be used for food, the interior should be finished with a smooth, food-safe glaze.

VARIATIONS

A DISH WITH CURVED BOTTOM AND EXTRUDED FOOT RING

The the same type of die used to create walls for the dish in the above project (fig. 9) can be used to make a dish with a press molded, curved bottom and extruded foot ring. Round and oval forms are more appropriate for this method. A found form such as a shallow metal or plastic dish can be used to make a plaster mold for the dish's curved

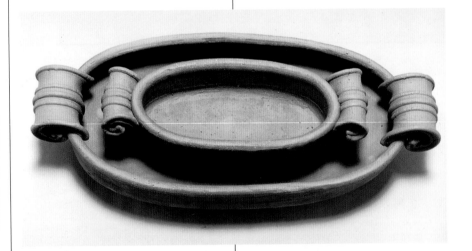

Three sizes of shallow oval press molds are used for making the bottoms of extruded dishes.

Slabs are coaxed into the shallow molds with a damp sponge or sand-filled sock.

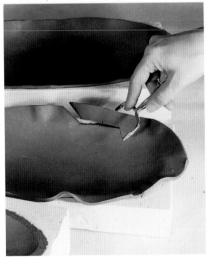

A cheese wire is used to trim away excess clay from the press molded bottom.

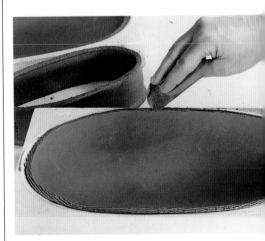

While still in the mold, the edge of the carved bottom is scored in preparation for joining it to an extruded wall.

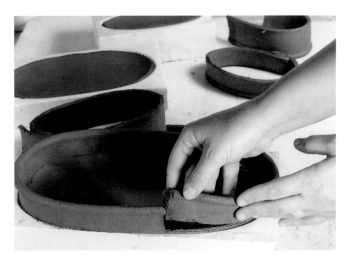

The extruded wall of a serving dish can be attached while its curved bottom remains in the plaster mold for support.

When the press molded bottom is stiff enough to hold its shape, an extruded foot is attached.

bottom. Found forms can be used two ways—to make hump (convex) or drape (concave) molds. To make a hump mold, begin by applying a releasing medium to the inside of a found form, then pour plaster directly into it. To make a drape (concave) mold, put the form inside a mold box or "coddles" (wood, tar paper, or a non-stick pan), and pour plaster around and over the form.

If you don't have found containers, modeled or thrown clay shapes can be cast in plaster to create shallow molds for the bottom of the dish. (If you're not familiar with mold making, refer to a comprehensive book on the subject.)

Attaching extruded walls to curved bottoms is done in the same manner as attaching walls to flat bottoms, but the

bottom's curve must be supported during building so that it doesn't flatten. The bottom can be left in the plaster mold while adding walls, or supported by foam placed underneath it during construction. After the walls are

attached, the dish is inverted onto its lip, an extruded foot ring is added, and the dish is turned right side up onto its foot. If the bottom is sufficiently stiff and the foot ring properly placed, the bottom's curve will remain.

The thumbnail line drawn equidistant from the edge of the bottom all around the dish is used to mark placement for the foot ring.

RANDY JOHNSTON, *Triangular Covered Form,* 1999. 6 x 6 x 6 inches (15 x 15 x 15 cm). Stoneware with fluxed kaolin slip; extruded, altered, and assembled; wood-fired to cone 10.
Photo by Peter Lee.

A Dish with Gallery and Lid

If you want to make a lidded dish, you can design a wall die (see figure 8, p. 69) which incorporates at its upper edge a gallery, or lip, to support a lid. A wall die with gallery must be carefully designed. The gallery on the extrusion can easily distort once the soft form is out of the extruder. Distortion can be controlled by designing the die for a minimal gallery extension, and by designing a thickening in the wall at the point where the gallery projects from the wall. Using stiffer clay for the extrusions will also help. Once the walls are extruded, you can minimize distortion by placing them on long supports, such as wooden boards, with the gallery extension hanging over one edge until they stiffen a little.

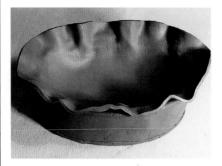

You can easily make a lid for a dish with a gallery by draping a soft slab of clay into the leather-hard dish. The dish must be bilaterally symmetrical or, when the lid is inverted, it won't fit. For a medium-sized dish, roll a ¼-inch-thick (6 mm) slab 3 inches (7.5 cm) larger all around than the dish's circumference.

Coax the slab into the dish, draping it downward to create an inverted dome shape. Lids can pose fit problems for a number of reasons. Lid depth can be deceptive when viewed from above—the lid will usually appear deeper than it is. The lid will seem to shrink more than the dish because it is constructed when the bottom has already begun to shrink; the lid will also flatten a little during firing. As you gain experience, you can counter these difficulties by creating a lid that is a little deeper and a little larger. Your experience will also inform the lid's shape—its curve can be a continuation of the wall, extending it in a smooth arc. The shape of the arc—how it rises and where it crests—will be a matter of your personal aesthetic.

Leave the lid to stiffen in the dish for an hour or two. Then lift it from the dish and, using a craft knife and Surform tool, cut and plane away excess clay from its edges. Proceed carefully, frequently trying the lid for size as you trim. If the lid is a bit soft, it can be made to fit more easily. A lid that is too large is better than one too small because of its continuing shrinkage—the damp lid is being fitted to a leather-hard form which has already shrunk.

When the lid fits well, place it on the dish, cover the construction in plastic, and let both parts stiffen overnight. You can add knobs or handles when the lid is stiff enough to support them. Handles and knobs are another opportunity to introduce your personal style into the work. Although knobs and handles can be any shape, their proportion and weight are an issue. Chapter 7 offers ideas on using extruded bands as handles.

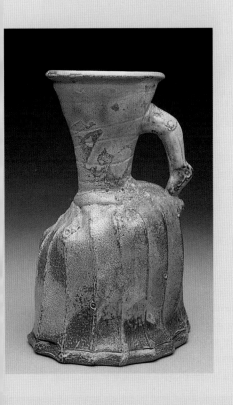

JOHN GLICK,
Vase with Handle, 1997.
8½ inches (21.25 cm)
high. Stoneware;
extruded and altered
body form with wheel-
thrown top; soda-fired
to cone 10 reduction.

BOWLS

Unlike baking dishes designed with flat bottoms for stability on an oven rack, bowls need a sloped or curved bottom to accommodate their use with spoons. Curved bottoms also increase their holding capacity. Bowl bottoms for extrusion construction can be slab built, thrown, or press molded.

SLAB BOTTOMS

One way to build a sloping bottom from a flat slab is to create a shallow cone. Begin by rolling and cutting a slab into a circle, then set it aside on a canvas-covered surface to stiffen for a few minutes. The examples shown in photo 2 are 6- and 7-inch-diameter (15 and 17.5 cm) circles about ⅛ inch (3 mm) thick. Cut and remove a wedge-shaped segment from the circle, bearing in mind that removing a larger segment will create a steeper cone. When you cut the wedge shape, remember that the join will have a larger cross section and will be stronger if you angle both cuts, so bevel-cut the join.

Next, roughen the cut edges with a serrated metal rib. At this point, the clay is soft enough that a single pass with the rib will slightly roughen the edge while preserving the integrity of the bevel. With a small brush, apply a little water to the edges that will be joined. (You want to soften only the edges, not the form.)

For a strong seam, one that will not open up through drying and firing, overlap the bevel-cut edges ¹⁄₁₆ inch (1.5 mm) when joining them, and press the seam against a canvas-covered surface. The join can be allowed to show if you prefer, or smoothed out with a rib or knife. Leaving process marks allows the user to see how the piece was made, and occasionally invites a metaphorical reading. For example, the line left in a bowl bottom might suggest the hand of a clock, a sundial, or a tinware seam, and present an interesting surprise when the bowl is emptied.

Once the join is made, invert the shallow cone onto a small piece of foam rubber to help it retain its shape. The cone will flatten if it's not supported. Allow the slab cone to stiffen before adding extruded components such as a foot ring or wall. If you're making a series of bowls or dishes, construct the slab parts and cover them with

plastic while extruding sections for foot rings and walls.

Because extrusions are narrow, they dry more quickly than slabs. If you're making multiple bowls or dishes, store extrusions on top of and under plastic to insure that the extrusions are optimally workable when you attach them to slabs. An occasional spritz with water will also keep them soft.

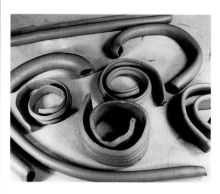

As you pull extrusions, circle them onto the table in the approximate diameter you will need. Bend them while they're still soft, but let them stiffen a little before attaching bottoms.

It is a good idea to work on foam rubber while attaching extruded walls to conical bottoms. The foam will protect the conical form from flattening. Once the walls are attached, the bowl can be turned onto its lip for placement of a foot ring (or you can attach the foot ring first and then add the walls). As

always, foot ring placement is important. If the foot is too small, the bowl will be unstable; if it is too large, the finished piece will look clumsy.

Extrusions from the same die, either at full height or cut down, can be used for both the foot ring and wall. If you want to alter the height of an extrusion—for example, narrow it for use as a foot ring—cut the extrusion when it is first pulled, then arrange it in a circle on your work surface. Or you can experiment and combine different extrusions on the same piece, changing from plain to fancy or thick to thin as the extrusions move around the bowl, creating a varied but useful wall and a playful but stable foot ring.

PRESS MOLDED BOTTOMS

Like the press molded bottoms used for making oval dishes earlier in this chapter, bowls with curved bottoms can also be constructed using press molded bottoms with extrusions as

walls, rims, feet, and handles. A bowl made this way will have greater holding capacity than one with a conical bottom, because the interior will be more rounded.

The difference between a curve-bottomed baking dish and a similarly made bowl is that the bowl can use both shallow and deep forms as press molds. The depth of form you press will depend on how much of the bowl's basic shape you wish to create with extrusion. Like baking dishes with curved bottoms, plaster forms for bowl bottoms can be created from found objects—plastic or metal dishes, or thrown or modeled clay forms—and used to create the bowl's basic shape. Techniques for attaching extrusions to press molded bowl bottoms are the same as for attaching walls to other forms with slab-built or pressed bottoms.

LEON POPIK,
Self Realization, 1993.
27 x 19 x 18 inches
(67.5 x 47.5 x 45 cm).
Stoneware (thrown pieces), stoneware and grog (extrusions); extruded and altered, wheel-thrown; cone 06, cone 9. Photo by artist.

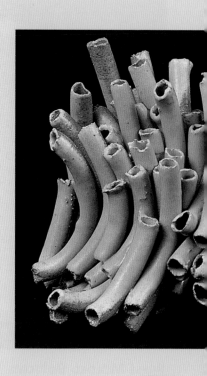

WHEEL-THROWN BOTTOMS

Wheel-throwing a bottom for a bowl offers some advantages. The bowl's depth and diameter can be easily varied and controlled, and throwing marks left on the piece can add to its overall visual appeal. There is a disadvantage, however, because you'll have to invert and trim the thrown bottom before adding the wall, foot ring, or other components. There's a ready argument for creating a bowl solely by wheel-throwing, which may be that it is more time efficient and, depending on your skill, easier than the process of hand-building combined with throwing. But efficiency is not the only issue. Creating forms that continue to challenge and interest the potter is also important.

Top: TRAUDI THORNTON, *Eliot's Flute*, 1998. 9 x 7½ x 13½ inches. (23 x 19 x 34 cm). Stoneware; extruded and assembled; reduction fired to cone 8. Photo by artist.

Center: MIKEL KELLEY, *Draper Dwellings*, 1998. 22 inches (55 cm) long. Stoneware; extruded with low-fire glazes and stains; cone 06. Photo by Eric Ferguson.

Bottom: RANDY JOHNSTON, *Teapot*, 1999. 8 x 9 x 7 inches (20 x 22.5 x 17.5 cm). Stoneware with fluxed kaolin slip; extruded, altered, and assembled; wood-fired to cone 10. Photo by Peter Lee.

EXTRUDED FOOT RINGS FOR BOWLS

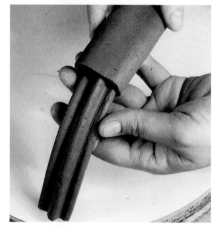

Regardless of its method of construction or size, a bowl with a curved bottom requires some sort of foot ring for support. A foot ring's placement affects both its stability and overall appearance. If the foot ring is too small and too close to the center of the bowl, it will be less stable. If it's placed too far from center, the bowl will be more stable, but perhaps less graceful. A compromise usually works best.

Placement of the foot ring is in part determined by the steepness of the bowl's curve. A shallow curve requires placement further from the center of the bowl's underside; if, on the other hand, the curve is steep, the foot ring can be positioned closer to the center. The rule of thumb is that the foot ring diameter be smaller than half and larger than a third of the diameter of the bowl. (This may be a personal preference. You can examine historical and contemporary examples and decide for yourself.)

The heft and height of the foot ring is partly a matter of personal choice. It's important to choose a scale for the foot that complements and continues other elements of the piece, and that maintains a hand-wrought ethos. Handcrafted ware usually has heavier, higher foot rings than are seen on industrially produced objects. Small feet on industrial ware are a result of the limits of a mechanized forming process. Allowing more light under a piece adds to its perceived volume. The undersized feet of industrial wares do keep the bottoms of objects off the table, but do not increase the pleasures of volume, shadow, and light.

CHAPTER SEVEN

EXTRUDED COILS AND BANDS

RINA PELEG, *Gold Art Structure*, 1993. 25 x 23 x 20 inches (62.5 x 57.5 x 50 cm). Low-fire yellow earthenware; extruded; cone 04. Photo by artist.

PREVIOUS CHAPTERS SHOW how solid extrusions can serve as supports and basic structural components. They can also, in the form of coils and bands (flattened coils), be used to structure and decorate works. Coils have been used to create and embellish clay vessels for centuries. And while they are traditionally and typically made by hand, coils can be created more evenly and efficiently by extrusion, and used for the same applications as are hand-formed coils.

In addition to taking you through the steps of creating a band-built pot with extruded bands, this chapter offers ideas and information on ways to create distinctive functional and sculptural works using the extruder's ability to produce coils and bands in quantities both small and large. Coils and bands can form parts of ware such as edges and rims, handles and feet, and applied decoration. When woven, or used to coil or band build, they can create the wares themselves.

RINA PELEG, *Brown Art #4*, 1986. 35 x 22 x 15 inches (87.5 x 55 x 37.5 cm). Brown clay; extruded and woven; cone 04. Photo by artist.

Top: PHILLIP SELLERS, *Signature #11*, 1998. 15 inches (37.5 cm) high by 8 inches (20 cm) in diameter. Stoneware; extruded and woven; cone 5.

Bottom: PHILLIP SELLERS, *Signature #3*, 1998. 9½ x 10 x 14 inches (23.75 x 25 x 35 cm). Stoneware; extruded and woven; cone 5. Photos by Jerry Anthony.

EXTRUDED PARTS

HANDLES

It is generally accepted that studio extrusion found its first use as a way to make handles. Using extruded coils has long been recognized as an efficient way to make handles, particularly for utilitarian production items and series of wares such as mugs, pitchers, and teapots. Figures 1 through 3 show a selection of various handle dies.

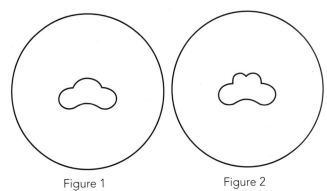

Figure 1   Figure 2

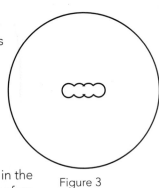

Figure 3

There are a few different approaches to using extrusion to make handles: Coils and coil variations can be used straight from the extruder "as is," or altered by pulling or hand-forming. The original method was to cut a segment of a simple extruded coil and "pull" it in the traditional manner, either before or after attachment to the object. Another approach is to bend and attach to the pot a coil or decorative band just as it is when it comes from the extruder. Extruded coils and bands can also be manipulated in ways other than pulling—for example, the end of a beaded handle can be split into sections and the sections curled at their points of attachment to the pot.

Whether round or flattened, extruded coils to be used for handles still benefit from a little shaping and tamping. Pulling narrows and flattens the bottom of the handle; tamping the upper end of the handle thickens it, and splays it out for easy attachment—a handle that's heftier at the upper join looks, and probably is, stronger.

Top: SHIRL PARMENTIER, *2-Sided Coil Vessel,* 1998. 12 x 24 x 8 inches (30 x 60 x 20 cm). Brown stoneware; extruded and assembled; reduction fired to cone 10. Photo by Ralph Gabriner.

Bottom: SHIRL PARMENTIER, *3-Sided Coil Vessel,* 1997. 16 inches 40 cm) high,17 inches (42.5 cm) in diameter. Brown stoneware; extruded and altered with slab base; reduction fired to cone 10. Photo by Allan Byr.

TODD TUREK, *Tray,* 1996. 3 x 7 x 19 inches (7.5 x 17.5 x 47.5 cm). Black stoneware; extruded sides, hand-built corners and slab bottom; cone 5. The use of extruded bands to frame the work enhances the design of this pleasing dish.

The handles and edges of these trays are formed with hollow extruded bands.

RIMS, EDGES, AND BEADS

Coils and bands can also be used to create the rims and edges of functional objects. The edges of slab-built ware often invite a frame or border that is easily created with an extruded band. Another way to neatly finish an edge is with a coil (or "bead") with a notch or slot running down its length, which facilitates easy attachment of the bead to the edge of a clay wall. (See fig. 12.)

Beads serve both structural and aesthetic functions: They thicken and reinforce the edges of objects, and can give a finished, accented look to the edges of your work. An added bead can be decorative, visually accentuating the edges of a clay work, like "piping" placed around the collar and cuffs of a garment.

When working with extruded beads, it's important to bear in mind the following considerations. An extruded bead must be pliable enough to bend and conform to the piece to which you are attaching it. The bead may shrink and crack if the difference between the bead's dampness and that of the clay body to which you are attaching it is too great. To attach a bead to an object, score and dampen the edge of the object, and place the slotted side of the bead over that edge. Run your fingers along the bead, squeezing gently to join it without distortion. If you wish, you can run a wooden

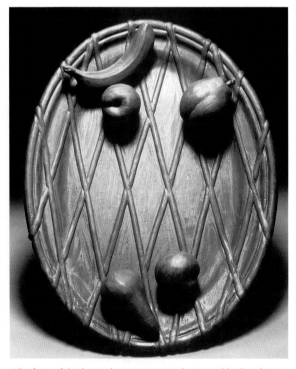

The form of this large platter was pressed on a mold taken from an extrusion-enhanced metal tray. The applied lattice decoration was extruded using a blockout die.

Bob Kinzie applies extrusions to the surfaces of his sculptural works to add textural interest.

STEPHANIE CIONCA, *Pot*,
1998. 16 inches (40 cm) tall.
Terra-cotta and sigilatta;
method used; cone 10.

wares. Another option is to cut chubby beaded coils into short lengths and use them as decorative "bun" feet, or furniture feet, on boxes and other items that don't need the full linear support of an extruded coil. Figures 4 through 6 show various foot dies.

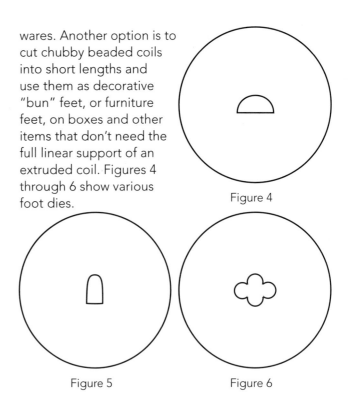

Figure 4

Figure 5

Figure 6

EXTRUSION AS STRUCTURE

COIL AND BAND BUILDING

Coil building has long been the method of choice for making large vessels, both historic and contemporary. The extruder's ability to produce flattened coils makes "band building," a modern variation of coil building, an excellent way to create large vessels that have historically been made with hand-rolled coils.

tool along the seam to seal the bead to the body, but you needn't worry about the attachment—the slotted fit, and shrinkage during drying guarantees the bead's adherence. Once attached, the bead can either be left untouched or manipulated—it can be angled, interrupted, pinched, tweaked, thinned, poked, or impressed. The ease of attachment leaves the bead with a clean line and a logical place to change glaze color, if that appeals to you. By waxing the bead, or waxing up to it during the glazing process, you can create a color change and a strong visual accent. Or, left the same color, the bead will create a pleasing structural accent.

FEET

Chapters 4 and 5 show how an extruded coil with a flattened side can make an efficient, stable, and beautiful foot ring for a platter, bowl, or baking dish. But a singular, plain coil is not the only solution for making a foot—many different extruded bands can be used singly or in combination to support utilitarian

PHYLLIS KUDDER-SULLIVAN, *Enigma Study 2*, 1997. 7½ x 14½ x 8½ inches (18.75 x 36.25 x 21.25 cm). Stoneware; extruded and woven; cone 6. Photo by Joseph D. Sullivan.

WOVEN STRUCTURE

Bands and coils can also be woven to create structures. Vessel forms such as baskets, bowls, and platters made with this technique are most often created by weaving and pressing soft coils inside a mold that both controls the form's shape and supports the coils while they are still soft. Weaving is done inside molds, rather than over them, because bands and coils dry quickly and are likely to shrink and crack if used over a hump mold. The appropriate size of coils and bands to use for weaving depends on the size of the object you are making. (Thin hollow tubes can also be woven.) Weaving can also be used in a more free-form manner, without molds, to create sculpture.

Top: JIM and SHIRL PARMENTIER, *Woven Clay Vessel*, 1998. 15 x 7 x 3 inches (37.5 x 17.5 x 7.5 cm). Brown stoneware; extruded and woven; reduction fired to cone 10.
Bottom: JIM and SHIRL PARMENTIER, *Woven Vessel*, 1998. Photos by Ralph Gabriner.

Top: ELINA BRANDT-HANSEN, *Fractal Formula*, 1998. 6¼ x 28 x 4¾ inches (16 x 70 x 12 cm). Colored stoneware and colored porcelain; extruded, wrapped, cut, and assembled.
Bottom: detail, *Fractal Formula*.
Photo by Rune Saevig.

Die Design for Coils, Bands, and Beads

Coils

Dies for coils are round holes created by variously sized drill bits—smaller bits for thinner coils, and larger bits for thicker coils. You might use thin coils for applied decoration, medium-sized coils for nubs from which to pull handles for mugs, and thick coils for additions to large vessels.

You can easily make your own dies for coils: Decide the size of the coil you want to make, select an appropriate drill bit, drill two or three same-sized holes (about an inch [2.5 cm] apart) near the center of a die blank, and *voila!*—you've got a die. (There's no need to bevel the holes.) If you want to extrude coils of different sizes, you can make separate dies for each size, or drill holes for two or three sizes in one die. You don't need many sizes to have a good variety for studio work—small (¼-inch [6 mm] bits), medium (⅜-inch [9 mm] bits), and large (½-inch [1.3 cm] bits) will probably satisfy most of your needs.

Some ready-made coil dies include several hole sizes in one die; each hole is used by blocking off those you don't want to extrude through. These can be a little awkward to use if there are many holes; getting the block-out piece in just the right place can prove tricky. As an alternative, you can make your own multiple coil die with three or four differently sized holes drilled far enough apart to comfortably allow selection of those you wish to use with your own block-out device. Figure 7 shows a multiple coil die; figure 8 shows a block-out die.

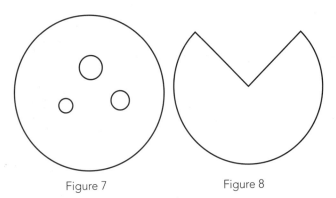

Figure 7   Figure 8

Bands

Dies for bands can be plain or fancy, smooth or textured, thick or thin. Plain bands are best for band building large pots. Band variations that include ovals, corrugated, and beaded shapes will find use as rims, feet, and decorative additions. Figures 9, 10, and 11 show a selection of band dies.

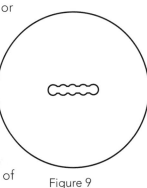

Figure 9

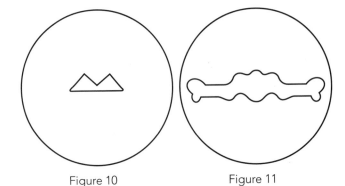

Figure 10   Figure 11

Decorative bands extruded using the die shown in fig.11.

Slotted Beads

A bead's intended use will determine the size of the die you design. If you are using it for large items with heavy walls, you will need to use a bigger bit to drill the die, and the notch will need to be larger to accommodate a heavier wall. For small and delicate objects, you will drill a smaller hole and create an appropriately scaled-down notch.

Since the use of extruded beads doesn't have a long history, and their possible uses remain unexplored, it's

up to you to discover ways to use them. Your dies might be more complex—a twin bead with a slot or, perhaps, a round bead angled and altered by filing. As in wheel-throwing, when an object's lip is slanted to reiterate the angle of the shoulder, beads can be designed for particular uses or altered to conform to aspects of the object to which they are attached.

Extruded, press molded, and wire-cut parts can be combined to create sculptural works.

Making a slotted bead die is easy. Using a ⅜-inch (9 mm) bit, drill a single hole into a die's center and add a small amount of epoxy putty to a small area on the inside of the drilled hole.

Once dry, the putty can be shaped into a V with a small hand file; the V protruding into the round hole will cause the length of the extrusion to be slotted.

Experimentation will help you discover your preferences for a slotted bead die's hole size and notch shape. Making beads

of a few different sizes in one die is an efficient way to experiment. (Three holes will not weaken the die too much.) Be careful, though, to locate the holes an inch (2.5 cm) or so apart from each other; using the one you want requires blocking the other holes with a piece of scrap plastic laid in place on top of the die. Or, if you wish, you can make a specific plastic block-out shape that can be laid on top of the die in the die holder. Figure 12 shows a simple notched bead die, while figure 13 shows a more decorative version; figure 14 shows a notched bead die that can be used for decorative purposes, or as a gallery die, to support the lid of a bowl or dish.

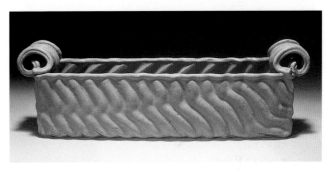

Slotted coils are used on edges to accentuate the rippled, textured surfaces of ware built from slabs.

BLOCK-OUT

Using a straight-sided plastic block-out with a beveled edge allows you to create another kind of decorative coil. Using standard coil dies, you can make flat-sided and half-round coils of various sizes and thicknesses. Instead of blocking out an entire die hole, a beveled plastic segment can block out only part of the hole—as much or as little as you wish. The resulting extrusion can be attached to the surface of wares to create thin, raised linear effects (applied decoration). Figure 15 shows an example of a block-out die.

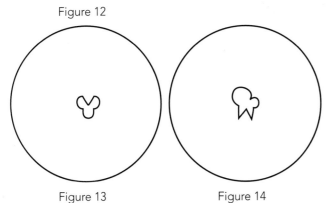

Figure 12

Figure 13

Figure 14

Figure 15

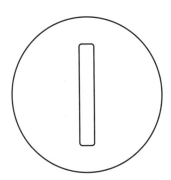

A LARGE BAND-BUILT POT

TO CREATE A POT LIKE THE ONE PICTURED, YOU WILL NEED:

25 POUNDS (11.35 KG) OF CLAY BODY

2 DIES (FIGS. 13 & 14, WHICH ARE WIDER AND NARROWER BANDS)

SHEETS OF NEWSPAPER

GARBAGE BAGS OR SHEETS OF PLASTIC

EXTRUDER

WOOD BOARD

PLASTIC BAT

SERRATED METAL RIB

POTTER'S KNIFE

BRUSH

SMOOTH METAL RIB

BANDING WHEEL (OPTIONAL)

HAIR DRYER OR HEAT LAMP (OPTIONAL)

WOODEN PADDLE

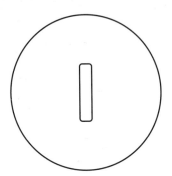

Figure 13

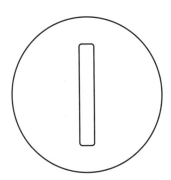

Figure 14

Bands for the project are extruded, placed in circles on a plastic bat, and covered, ready for building.

1 Begin by extruding approximately 12 lbs. (5.5 kg) of clay. (If you are using a 4-inch [10 cm] extruder, this will be one full barrel's worth.) Use a 2-inch-wide (5 cm) die for three quarters of the extrusions, and a 1-inch-wide (2.5 cm) die for the remaining extrusions. Cover a wood board in a sheet of plastic, then arrange the extrusions in loose concentric circles on the plastic-covered board. Cover the extrusions with plastic. Set these aside temporarily while you roll the slab, next.

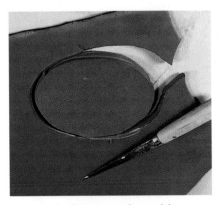

A bottom for the pot is cut from a slab.

2 Roll a small ⅜-inch-thick (9 mm) slab, and from it cut a circle 5 to 7 inches (12.5 to 17.5 cm) in diameter; this will serve as the bottom of your pot. Lay a piece of paper on your plastic bat, then place the slab circle on the paper-covered bat.

Score and dampen the edge of the bottom in preparation for the addition of the first band.

3 Use a serrated rib to score the edge of the slab circle, and dampen the edge with water. Next, score the edge of an extrusion and join it to the slab circle; bevel-cut and score the ends of the extrusion to join it around the slab's circumference. Notice that this first band stands straight up, leaning neither in nor out.

Angling the edges of bands, as pictured, will cause the pot to swell outward.

4 To make the pot begin to curve outward, angle the upper edge of the first attached band with your knife. Angle the knife downward toward the outside of the pot and run it around the band at about a 15° angle, pressing lightly. Now score that angled edge with a serrated rib and dampen (just the edge) with a brush and water (do not use a spray bottle). Score the next extrusion and place it on top of the first. This extrusion will tip out slightly because, although it's bottom edge is straight, the one under it has been tilted. Press the extrusion in place, then cut and join the ends.

The pot grows slowly outward with the addition of each succeeding band.

5 With the next addition, the extrusion will be added in two pieces, roughly halves. Proceed as in

step 4. Angle the top edge of the extrusion already in place, and score and add the next extruded band. Cut, score, and join the extrusions' ends.

At this point, the pot will need to be stiffened a little before proceeding with the addition of more extruded bands.

6 Now move the bat and the pot to a surface a little lower than table height, perhaps onto a stool next to your table. If you are using a banding wheel, place the bat on the wheel at this point; if you don't have a banding wheel, you can walk around the pot backwards as you work—the traditional method of working on large vessels. You need to be above the pot for this step. Using your smooth metal rib on the outside of the pot, stroke the rib up and across the lowest horizontal seam at a 45° angle, supporting the wall on the inside with your other hand. Proceed all the way around the pot, scraping evenly upward and diagonally. A little clay will be dragged up and into the seam, smoothing it.

7 Proceed to the next higher seam, scraping upward diagonally across it, as in step 6.

8 Now focus your attention on the inside of the pot, scraping upward and diagonally across the interior seams (one at a time) with the metal rib, while supporting the wall with your outside hand.

9 At this point, if the walls are too soft to support the addition of more bands, stop and stiffen the wall a little with a hair dryer. (You can use a heat lamp or fan as long as the pot is stiffened evenly all the way around.) When the wall has stiffened but is still wet enough to accept new extrusions, you can add more bands as in step 4.

10 Continue working on your pot, adding extrusions, scraping, and stiffening (when needed). When you have completed about half the height of the pot, you can gently paddle your pot with a wooden paddle to smooth the walls. At some point, depending on the size of your pot, you may have to wrap it in plastic and put it away to stiffen overnight before you continue building.

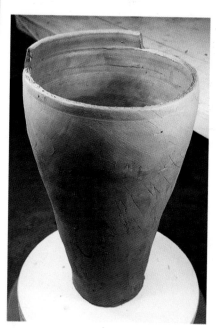

To angle the wall of the pot inward, make the upper edge of extrusions level for a row or two.

11 After you have added four or five layers of extrusion, you will begin to change the direction of swell of your pot by changing the angle of horizontal joins, first to level, then tilting inward. When your wall begins to angle inward, you will find it easier to work with narrower extrusions.

Changing the angle of the top edges turns the pot wall inward. Narrow extrusions work better for this section of the pot.

The neck of the pot grows from the shoulder, rather than shifting direction abruptly.

The pot must be stiffened at this point, before adding the weight of a neck and lip to the soft shoulder.

12 Most large pots can be built in three stages (with some time or stiffening in between): bottom half, middle and shoulder, and neck/lip. The shoulder must be stiffened before adding the weight of the neck and lip onto it. When adding a neck to your pot, whether short or tall, pay attention to the angle at which it meets the shoulder. A sudden sharp turn may be out of character with the swelling curves of the rest of the form. Also, remember that a big pot probably needs a lip of a size in keeping with its scale. Taking a close look at historical pots for guidance will help you with these subtle issues as well as with notions of proportion, curve, and decoration.

13 When your pot is complete and still damp, you can give it a final scraping or paddling to refine the form and surface. If your first band-built pot isn't perfect or reveals its construction bands, don't be discouraged. Some applied decoration or bold pattern will mask any imperfections, and your second big pot will be easier and better. You will discover the satisfaction of this method of working when you see what a large, voluminous, handsome, and amazingly lightweight vessel you have made in such a short time.

Top: YOUNG LEE, *Pot*, 1997. 12 x 9 inches (30 x 22.5 cm). Maiolica; extruded and band-built; cone 04.

Bottom: NANCY STOLL, *Mesopotamian Fertility Pot*, 1998. 18 inches (45 cm) long. Terra-cotta, stained and glazed. Photo by Diana Pancioli.

CHAPTER EIGHT

CONSTRUCTION WITH TWO- AND THREE-SIDED AND CURVED DIES

JOHN GLICK, *Tray*, 1997. 25 x 14 inches
(62.5 x 35 cm). Stoneware; extruded and
altered; reduction fired to cone 10.
Photo by artist.

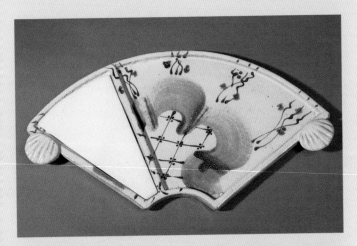

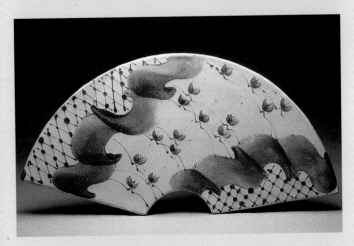

Top: JOHN GLICK, *Lidded Box*, 1997. 15 x 4¾ inches (37.5 x 11.9 cm). Stoneware; extruded base, lid, and feet; reduction fired to cone 10. Photo by artist.

Center: I.B. REMSEN, *Sushi Fan*, 1982. 12 x 8 inches. Stoneware with opaque glaze and copper-red overglaze; extruded off-center and assembled; cone 10 reduction. Photo by artist.

Bottom: I.B. REMSEN, *Arcing Rose Plaque*, 1984. 18 inches (45 cm) long. Stoneware with opaque glaze and copper-red overglaze; extruded off-center; cone 10 reduction. Photo by artist.

TWO- AND THREE-SIDED dies comprise a category midway between solid and fully hollow dies. Whereas the single shapes of solid dies and the two concentric shapes, or cutouts, of hollow dies have three or more sides (if geometric) or make a full circle (if round), the dies discussed in this chapter have only two or three sides, whether geometric or curved.

Two- and three-sided dies, like hollow dies, need a few U-bolts to support their center pieces and keep them from bending during use. The extrusions they make are more difficult to handle than solid or hollow forms, because their shapes when soft and fresh from the extruder, must usually be maintained by some type of support. They can be designed so that the extrusions they produce are thicker at critical

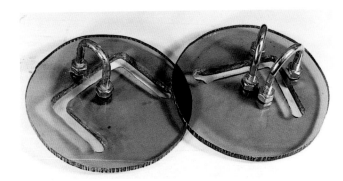

Photo 1

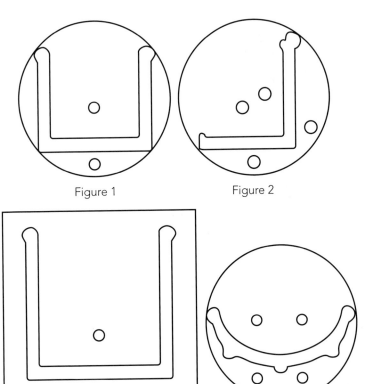

Figure 1   Figure 2

Figure 3   Figure 4

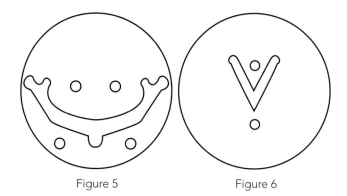

Figure 5   Figure 6

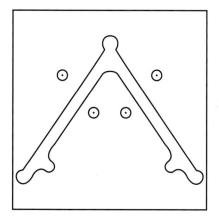

Figure 7

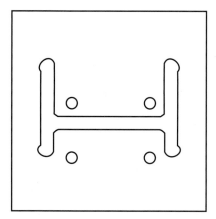

Figure 8

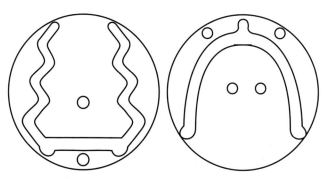

Figure 9   Figure 10

places (at corners and turns), and the forms can be extruded with slightly stiffer clay.

Two- and three-sided dies can be used to produce a variety of functional objects as well as sculpture. This chapter takes a look at box dies with two and three sides, drawings of which—along with variation dies and dies to create lids and other parts—are shown on this page. Making the actual projects in this chapter won't require using all the dies shown, but you may want to use those that you won't need for projects for some of the variations described below, or for works you make on your own. Photo 1 shows a two-sided and a three-sided box die for a 4-inch round-barreled extruder. Figures 1 and 2 provide actual die design drawings. Figures 3 through 10 show a variety of different two- and three-sided dies, most of which will be required or discussed later in the chapter.

Some forms made with two- and three-sided dies need support when first taken from the extruder. Some do not.

Frigures 5 and 9, when extruded, create a box and lid. Notice the lid flanges that make a positive fit with the box form.

DIE DESIGN FOR A THREE-SIDED BOX

(Note: The dies shown in figure 1 and figure 2 produce extrusions that include both the walls and bottom of a box. Using other dies, you can also separately extrude the bottom and walls for a box, or you can extrude the walls and slab roll the bottom. Although these dies produce straight walls, box walls do not have to be straight. Many potters create interesting boxes with curved and beaded wall dies, stiffening and mitre-cutting these extrusions as in standard slab construction.)

The geometric U-shaped die shown in figure 1 is a three-sided box die, which you will use to create the project that follows. It is important to know that the limitations posed by the dimensions of extruder barrels are of particular concern when using a two- or three-sided die to extrude forms for a box. In the case of a round 4-inch barrel, the extrusion will be limited to a 3-inch die area; for a 5-inch barrel, the limit will be a 4-inch area. One or two U-bolts fitted to link the die's interior and exterior shapes will support the interior of the U shape and keep it from flexing under the pressure of the clay.

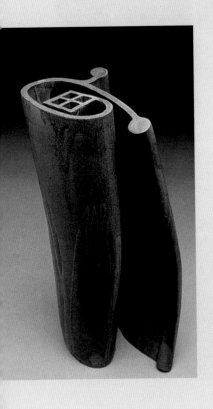

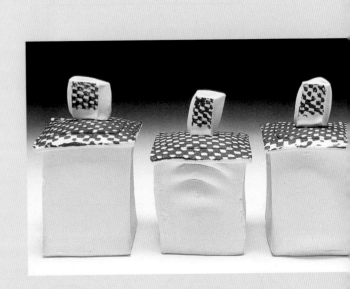

Top: PAUL LEWING, *Card Holder*, 1985. 2½ inches (6.25 cm) high. Porcelain; extruded.

Center: PAUL LEWING, *Soap Dishes*, 1998. 3 x 5 x 1 inches (7.5 x 12.5 x 2.5 cm). Porcelain; extruded and hand-cut to a template; cone 5.
Photos by Paul Schreiber.

Bottom: FRANK BOSCO, *Vase*, 1998. Stoneware; extruded; cone 10 reduction.
Photo by artist.

D. HAYNE BAYLESS, *Three Jars*. 5 x 3 x 3 inches (12.5 x 7.5 x 7.5 cm). Porcelain; extruded bodies with slab tops and lid knobs; reduction fired to cone 10. Photo by artist.

THE MATERIALS AND TOOLS LISTED BELOW
PERTAIN TO THE TWO BOX PROJECTS THAT
FOLLOW—A BOX WITH WRAPPED ENDS,
AND ONE WITH BUTT ENDS AND HANDLES.

12 LBS. (5.4 KG) OF CLAY BODY
(6 LBS EACH)

TWO DIES: THE DIE SHOWN IN FIG. 1,
AND ONE DECORATIVE BAND DIE

A FEW INCHES OF DRIED CLAY COILS
OF DIFFERENT THICKNESSES

EXTRUDER

2 WOOD BOARDS 1 x 3 x 24 INCHES
(2.5 x 7.5 x 60 CM)

POTTER'S KNIFE

SERRATED RIB

WATER AND BRUSH

1 Using the figure 1 die, extrude two lengths of clay, each 12 to 14 inches (30 to 35 cm).

2 If the extrusions need straightening, press wood boards against their sides, inside and out. Cut in a straight or curved line and remove a 3-inch (7.5 cm) bottom section from both ends of one extrusion. While the extrusion is still soft, score and wrap the protruding wall flaps—first one, then the other—around the remaining bottom forms at both ends.

3 Decide how you would like to join the wrapped ends. They can be bevel-cut, scored, joined, and smoothed to hide the seam, or they can be scored and lapped. It is best not to lap a large amount, as that will add unnecessary weight to the box. A dried coil pin broken to a length of ¾ inch (1.9 cm) can be inserted into the join for a decorative effect.

VARIATIONS

A BOX MADE WITH A TWO-SIDED DIE

To overcome the limitation of a 4-inch (10 cm) barrel and create a larger box, you can make one die (see fig. 2) which will extrude one side and one half of the bottom of a box. These L-shaped extru-

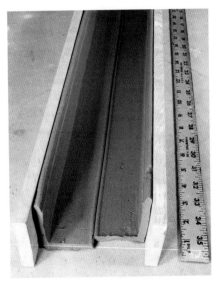

PROJECT

A BOX WITH BUTT ENDS

1 This box can be more easily constructed when the extrusion has stiffened a little; follow steps 1 and 2 for the wrapped box project above, but allow the extrusions to stiffen before working with them. Then, with a sharp knife, cut a 4-

inch length from one end of the extrusion, and trim the other end of the extrusion. The 4-inch segment will form both ends of the box. Cut away the walls from the bottom on both sides of the 4-inch segment, then trim and butt-join these pieces to each end of the box.

2 Extrude about 20 inches (50 cm) of decorative band and cut it into 4- to 5-inch (10 to 12.5 cm) lengths. Practice curling the lengths into handles, and choose the two best to attach to the ends of your box. Score and dampen the handles, then press them in place.

sions can be joined down the center bottom to make a larger box—about 3½ inches (8.75 cm) wide and of whatever length you desire. The L-shaped extrusion is pulled, straightened, and stiffened a little before it is joined to its other half. Note: Like the three-sided box die, this die also needs u-bolt support.)

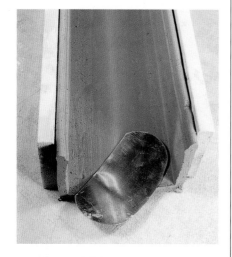

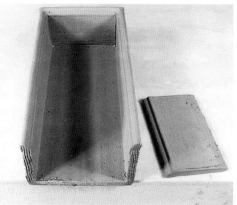

To join the two L-shaped extrusions, score and dampen the center bottom edges, then place the pieces closely beside each other in a mirror image fashion. Press down on the seam first with your finger and then with a smooth metal rib. The extrusion can be designed with a thickening at the center edge to add clay to the seam. You can wrap the ends (see step 3, A Box with Wrapped Ends) if the extrusions are damp enough, or construct ends with butt-edge segments cut from another piece of extrusion. The larger dimensions of this box make it useful for a wide variety of items. You can add handles or a lid if your plans for its function require them.

BUTTER DISHES

A three-sided box die or curved lid die, inverted and redesigned, can become a butter dish cover (see fig. 10). You can take liberties with this form as long as the cover sits firmly in its tray (and the butter fits!). The butter cover's ends, like box ends, can be wrapped, constructed, or pinched. A die can be made with an extruded protrusion on top that acts as a handle and extends the full length of the cover or it can be partially cut away. Or, if you prefer a cover without a handle, you can design a die to produce a ribbed or textured surface that will both give you a good grip on the cover and add visual interest to the piece.

A 4-inch (10 cm) barrel can't extrude a flat tray shape large enough to accommodate the butter dish cover that the same-sized extruder can make. But if you design a tray that is slightly curved and then let it slump to level when it comes out of the extruder, it will be just wide enough to serve as a tray for the butter cover (see fig. 4). This tray will need extra feet to hold its bottom straight when it slumps—three or four beads drilled at intervals across the bottom width of the die profile will add feet to the extruded tray.

A large ear of corn was oiled and pressed into soft clay. The clay impression was fired to biscuit temperataure to serve as a press mold for a butter dish cover.

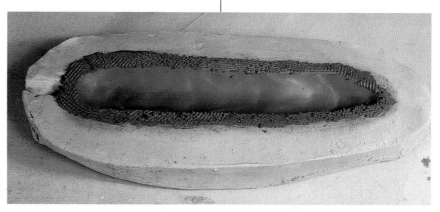

A clay slab is pressed into the biscuit mold to make the top of the butter dish cover

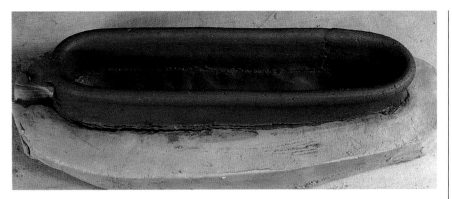

Extruded sides are added to the press molded butter dish top while it is still in the mold.

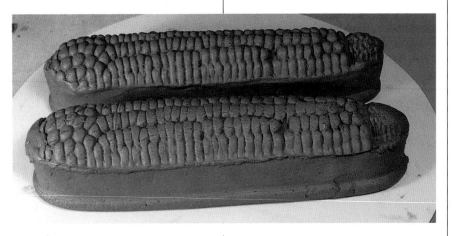

Two butter dish covers with corn impressions stiffen while their trays are being made.

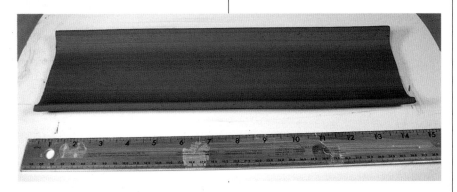

Extrusions to create trays for butter dishes are pulled, allowing extra length to form ends.

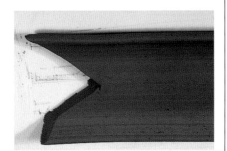

The ends of the extruded tray are darted and joined.

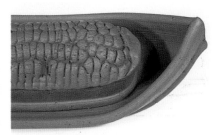

The length of the butter dish cover is fitted to the length of the tray.

BOX LIDS

Box lids can be made with curved, faceted, or V-shaped dies. A gallery to insure lid fit must be designed into the box die or into the lid die. Figures 6 and 7 show dies for box lids.

Curved extrusions pose a problem in that they flex when damp; in order to hold their curve, they must be supported. Often the diameter of that support determines the ultimate dimension of the lid. In other words, the arc of a damp curved extrusion can be compressed or expanded by its support. You can use various sizes of rolling pins, dowels, and

You can stiffen the curved section on a rounded support and, while the extrusion is still damp and somewhat flexible, fit it onto the box. The gallery of the box or lid is important because it holds the damp lid in its final shape. The gallery must be large enough to make a very positive fit with the box as they stiffen and dry together. Both pieces should be at a damp, leather-hard stage when the lid is fit so that the two pieces shrink simultaneously as they dry.

foam pipe insulation to support and alter the same curved extrusion to fit various widths of extruded boxes.

Segments cut from the side or lid extrusions are fitted, joined, and trimmed to create the ends of the lid.

The lid extrusion can be placed on top of the upside down box extrusion (right) until the box walls are stiff enough to hold the weight of the lid without collapsing. When both have stiffened, the box can be turned upright and the lid can be fitted to the box.

Curved lids don't hold their form as well as faceted shapes. This can be both an advantage and a disadvantage. As mentioned above, the same curved lid can be made to fit boxes of various widths, but it takes both time and timing to properly execute these variations. A V-shaped lid holds its shape a little better as it comes from the extruder, but still needs support (see fig. 7). Extruded forms like these can be thickened at strategic places—namely, where they change direction—to help them hold their shape.

99

SCULPTURAL SUPPORT

As well as being used to make boxes, extrusions from a three-sided, U-shaped die can be used to construct an understructure for wall sculpture; the structure increases depth without adding too much weight. Multiple U-shaped extrusions, joined side by side, will support slab work built over the structure. A double T-shaped extrusion can also be used for this purpose.

Jim Robison designed this double-T-shaped extruder die to make the understructure for his sculptural wall works.

The extrusions are straightened with boards before being joined.

An extruded support structure for a large wall piece is ready for the application of slabs.

Slabs have been applied to the extruded structure to create the surface of the wall sculpture.

Top left and right: JIM ROBISON, Detail, *Success is a Journey, Not a Destination*, 1995. 4 x 6 feet (120 x 180 cm). Stoneware; extruded understructure with slab additions; cone 8 reduction. Installation at Yorkshire Purchasing Organization in Wakefield, West Yorkshire, England.

Bottom: Jim Robison places leather-hard slabs over an extruded framework while working on *My Liverpool Home* (6 x 6 feet [15 x 15 cm],1999). Extrusions are also used to finish edge details.

CHAPTER NINE

CONSTRUCTION WITH ROUND AND SQUARE HOLLOW DIES

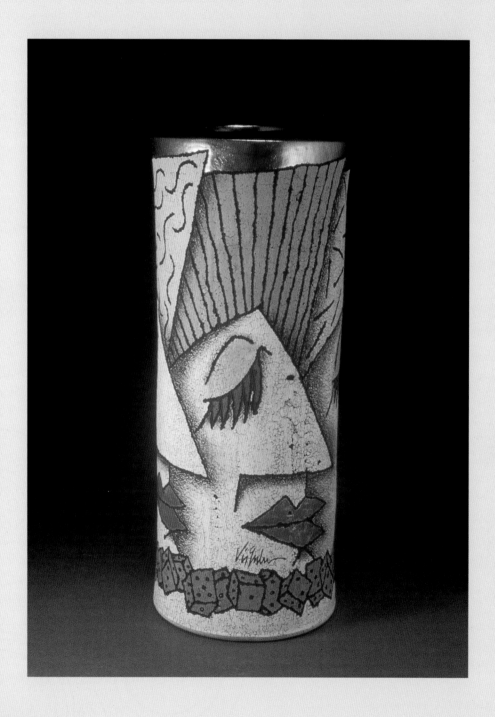

RIMAS VISGIRDA, *Vase*,
1992. 8 x 20 inches (20 x 50 cm);
Stoneware with white englobe;
extruded and altered;
cone 10, 05, 018.

WHILE SOLID EXTRUSIONS are interesting and useful, hollow extrusions carry a special fascination. With their volumes already formed as they exit the extruder, they seem to challenge you to make something with them. Hollow extrusions can be made in a variety of round, square, faceted, and other shapes to create utilitarian and other works in clay—cups and boxes, vases and umbrella stands, sculpture, and more.

This chapter offers ideas, information, and inspiration for working with hollow extrusions made from an array of differently shaped dies. The following pages also take you through two step-by-step projects—one using a round hollow die to make a ewer (a pitcher or cruet with no handle), and another using a square hollow die to create a vase.

HOLLOW ROUND DIES

Small- and medium-sized hollow round dies can be used to extrude clay forms for drinking vessels and vases; larger ones produce extrusions that work well for umbrella stands and different types of architectural forms. Making cups and vases from

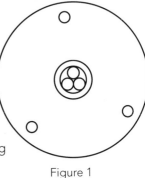

Figure 1

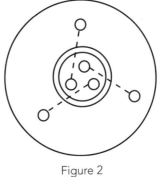

Figure 2

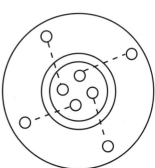

Figure 3

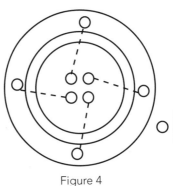

Figure 4

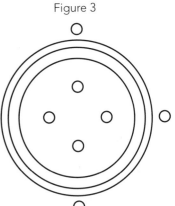

Figure 5

Top: WALTER KEELER, *Toast Machine*, 1998. 16 x 19 x 15 inches (40 x 47.5 x 37.5 cm). White earthenware; Extruded with additions, base thrown and altered; cone 01, 04.

Bottom: WALTER KEELER, *Toast Machine*, 1998. Earthenware; extruded on thrown base; cone 01, 04. Photos by artist.

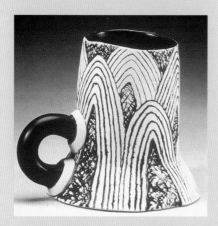

Top: RIMAS VISGIRDA, *Mug and Saucer*, 1992. Stoneware with white englobe; extruded and altered; cone 10, 05, 018.

Center: HARRIS DELLER, *Untitled Cup*, Volume Series with Concentric Arches, 1998. 4 x 5 x 4 inches (10 x 12.5 x 10 cm). Porcelain; wheel-thrown with extruded handle and jussets; cone 10 reduction. Photo by Jeff Bruce.

Bottom: RICHARD BURKETT, *Pair of Wood-Fired Cups*, 1997. Each cup 3 x 3 x 2½ inches (7.5 x 7.5 x 6.25 cm). Porcelain; extruded body (using computer-designed dies), slab base, press molded feet and handles; cone 11-12. Photo by artist.

extruded clay tubes is easy and fun—the objects themselves offer further proof of the variations extrusion can inspire. Figures 1 through 5 show a variety of small, medium, and large hollow round dies that can be used to make a variety of works in clay.

Cups

With the addition of a bottom and a handle, an extruded clay tube easily becomes a simple cup. But why stop there? Adding a decorative extruded band can give an interesting lip to the tube cup or, attached instead to the bottom (flush with the tube or indented), can serve as a decorative foot for the vessel. The same or a different band can be used as a handle.

Another type of extruded cup can be made using the "dart and tuck" method, by slightly altering the cup's tubular form and creating an angular projection that invites a handle. The clay tube can also be slit vertically, and a decorative band inserted in the slit, to broaden the cup and add formal and textural interest.

Extruded handles and decorative bands have been added at foot and lip to these hollow extruded cups.

These cups, made from hollow extruded tubes, have decorative extruded lips and pulled handles.

HOLLOW HANDLES

To keep a hollow extrusion from buckling and cracking as you bend and form it into a handle, you can cut a leaf-shaped segment out of the tube lapping the edges and bending the segment around a wooden dowel or brush handle. Because the tube must be bent when the extrusion is fresh out of the extruder, only a very sharp blade will cut the tube without squashing it—a craft knife or a sharpened potter's knife works best.

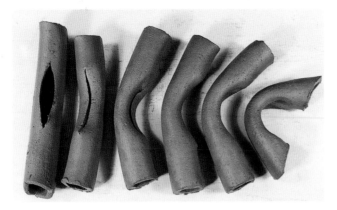

The stages of cutting and bending a freshly extruded hollow tube for use as a handle

DIANA PANCIOLI, *Teapot*, 1989. 8 x 8 x 5 inches (cm). Stoneware; extruded; salt-fired to cone 10 reduction. Photo by artist.

VASES

Potters love the vase shape because it allows so much design flexibility. Vases can be general or particular in design, designed for one or many flowers; for specific flowers (like Dutch *tulipieres* or Japanese Ikebana); for flowers long- or short-stemmed, slender or bushy, brightly or quietly colored. Vase forms, of course, can be other than round tubes; many shapes can contain water and support flowers.

Top: ROBERT HARRISON, *White Arch Sculptural Basket*, 1984. 10 x 15 x 6 inches (25 x 37.5 x 15 cm). Earthenware with terra sigilattas; extruded; salt-fired to cone 1.
Bottom: ROBERT HARRISON, *Dark Arch Sculptural Basket*, 1984. 10 x 15 x 6 inches (25 x 37.5 x 15 cm). Helmer clay; extruded; wood-fired to cone 10.

SPOUTED FORMS

Spouted forms such as teapots or ewers are visually and technically complex forms with numerous attachments and additions: spouts, handles, lids, knobs, and feet. They present the potter with an enjoyable challenge.

Top: FRANK BOSCO, *Vase*, 1998. 15 x 6 x 5 inches (37.5 x 15 x 12.5 cm). Stoneware; extruded; cone 10 reduction. Photo by Les Helmers.

Center: NILS LOU, *Vase*, 1989. 6 x 17 inches (15 x 42.5 cm). Stoneware; wheel-thrown body with extruded and altered neck; cone 10 reduction.

Bottom: GINNY CONROW, *Torso Vase*, 1998. 14 x 3 x 3 inches (35 x 7.5 x 7.5 cm). Porcelain; extruded, cut, and altered. Cone 10. Photo by Roger Schreiber.

Top: JOHN GLICK, *Teapot*, 1997. 5½ inches (13.75 cm) high. Stoneware; extruded, altered spout; cone 10 reduction. Photo by artist.

Bottom: HARRIS DELLER, *Untitled, Curvilinear Teapot with Passive Spout, Concentric Lines, Triangles, and Dots*, 1998. 13 x 10 x 3 inches (32.5 x 25 x 7.5 cm). Porcelain; wheel-thrown and altered with extruded handle and spout; cone 10 reduction. Photo by Jeff Bruce.

Teapots continue to be a favorite among potters, despite the fact that the advent of the tea bag has greatly reduced their use. Historically, potters have made ewers—pitchers with a neck and pouring spout, and sometimes a handle—for serving cold liquids. Although they are not designed to store liquids, they are sometimes fitted with lids or stoppers. Ewers can be large or small depending on the liquid they are designed to serve—wine, oil, vinegar, sauce, or other. Unlike teapots holding hot liquids, ewers don't need handles to protect the user from heat—a form that affords a comfortable grip is enough. While extruded tubes can be used to construct teapot and ewer bodies, they present a distinct problem. Although an extruded clay tube is volumetric, it doesn't have the pleasing roundness of a wheel-thrown form. A "dart and tuck" (dart and join) technique can be used to overcome an extruded tube's lack of roundness; the necks and spouts of teapots and ewers can also be shaped using this method. Triangular shapes (darts) are cut from the edges of a clay tube, the dart's edges are joined, and the dart point is softened by a little paddling. A dart creates a protrusion—a natural place to attach a spout, lug, or handle.

SPOUTS

Using a relatively simple technique, a variety of spouts—long and short, thick and thin—can be made from extruded clay tubes. To narrow a hollow tube to make a spout, you can cut a V-shaped segment (a dart) from one end with a sharp knife; score and dampen the edges of the dart, then press them together. After sealing the seam with a knife blade or smooth rib, you can further shape the tube by bending it. Variously sized tubes can be used depending on the size of the object for which they are designed. Darted spouts can also be used in reverse, with the small end attached to the pot. If you are making

Top: WALTER KEELER, *Teapot,* 1998. 9 inches (22.5 cm) high. Earthenware; extruded parts; cone 01, 04. Photo by Tony May.

Bottom: JOHN GLICK, *Ewers,* 1997. 8½ inches (21.25 cm) high. Stoneware; extruded and altered; cone 10 reduction. Photo by artist.

Using a very sharp knife, a dart is cut from the end of a freshly extruded tube.

multiples of a spouted form, a series of spouts can be quickly made and stored under plastic while you create the bodies of the teapots, ewers, or pitchers.

For variety, spouts can be twisted. Inserting a pencil or brush handle in the tube will prevent it from collapsing while you twist it with your hand. This same technique—supporting the tube with a dowel—can be used to texture hollow extrusions before they are dart-formed into spouts.

A variety of spout lengths created for a series of ewers

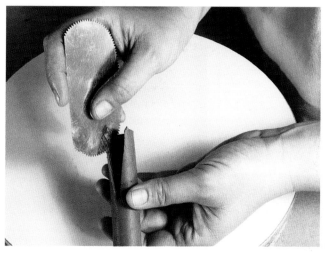

The edges of the dart are lightly scored with a serrated rib, and then dampened.

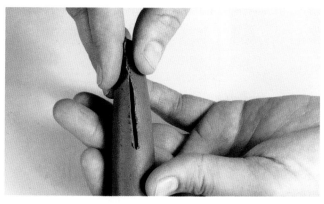

Gentle pressing on the sides of the tube will join the seam.

The tube can be bent to from a curved spout.

DIANA PANCIOLI, *Ewer*, 1989. 7 x 6 x 4 inches. Stoneware; extruded; reduction fired to cone 10. Photo by artist.

OPEN TUBES

Hollow tubes can be slit length-wise with a knife, opened flat, and lightly rolled for use as slab bottoms and tops for your tubular constructions. Or you can reform cylinders from the slabs, in the direction perpendicular to the way they were extruded, to create cylinders larger in diameter than your extruder barrel would allow. Opened tubular extrusions can be textured before being reconstructed into cylindrical bodies.

The cylinder on the right has the maximum diameter a 4-inch-barreled extruder can make. On the left, a larger cylinder was formed by cutting open a tube of the same diameter and reforming it in a direction perpendicular to the way it was extruded.

PROJECT
A EWER

TO MAKE A EWER LIKE THE ONE SHOWN, YOU WILL NEED:

10 LBS. (4.54 KG) OF CLAY BODY

EXTRUDER

3 HOLLOW ROUND DIES: SMALL (FIG. 1), MEDIUM (FIG. 3), AND LARGE (FIG. 5)

SHARP POTTER'S OR CRAFT KNIFE

PLASTIC GARBAGE BAGS OR SHEETS OF PLASTIC

A SHEET OF CANVAS

BRUSH

SERRATED RIB

SMOOTH RIB (OPTIONAL)

1 Using your large die, extrude a clay tube 18 inches (45 cm) long and approximately 3 inches (7.5 cm) in diameter. With a sharp knife, cut this extrusion into 6-inch (15 cm) segments. Next, use the medium die to extrude a clay tube 6 inches (15 cm) long; lay this extrusion down on your work surface, and cover it with plastic. Last, use the small die to extrude a clay tube 12 inches (30 cm) long; as you did with the medium-sized extrusion, lay this on your work surface and cover it with plastic.

2 Select the small extrusion. Following the process described in the Spouts section of this project (page 106), use it to make a 3½ inch (8 cm) spout or two. (The ewer will only need one spout, but there is enough clay tube to practice and experiment.) Cover these with plastic for now.

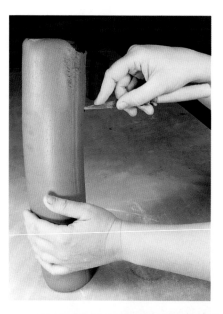

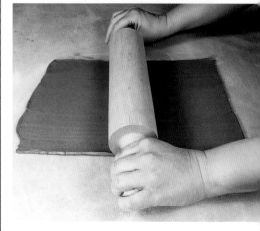

3 Select one of the 6 inch (15 cm) segments you cut in step 1, and use a sharp knife to slit it open lengthwise. Lay the slit segment on a canvas-covered surface, and lightly roll it (This will form the ewer's bottom.) Trim the bottom of a 6 inch (15 cm) tubular body segment to make it level, and stand it on the rolled slab.

4 Close-cut the slab around and ⅛ inch (3 mm) outside the tube's circumference at an angle. Use a serrated rib, brush, and water to score, dampen, and attach the tube to its slab bottom.

5 Shape the ewer's body, cutting a dart or two into the top edge of the tube about 1½ inches (3.8 cm) deep and 1 inch (2.5 cm) wide.

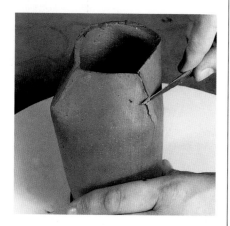

6 Score, dampen, and join the dart seams; use the flat side of a knife blade to smooth the seams.

7 Pinch a tiny piece of clay at the dart's upper edge to reinforce the seam.

8 With a sharp knife, trim the top of the tube to level.

9 From the remaining rolled clay slab, cut a small circle approximately 4 inches (10 cm) in diameter, with a V-shaped dart 1 to 1½ inches (2.5 to 3.75 cm) wide. Score and join the dart edges to form a cone.

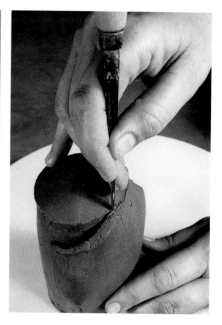

10 Wet the edge of the tubes with a brush and place the cone gently on top. The tube edge will leave a wet mark on the underside of the cone when you lift it away, showing you where to cut the cone for a good fit. Score the tube and the edges of the cone, attach the cone to the tube, and trim away any excess clay. Smooth the join with a knife edge.

11 Select the spout you like best from those you made in step 2, and (without actually attaching it) "fit" it to the body. To fit the spout—find its best placement, length, and angle of rise—hold it near the ewer's body, making sure that the bottom lip of the spout extends above the body's fill line for liquid.

12 When you have determined where the spout will be attached, cut a hole the size of the spout hole in the body, score the body and spout, then dampen and attach them.

13 From the medium-sized tubular extrusion, cut a segment approximately 1 to 2 inches (2.5 to 5 cm) tall. This will serve as the ewer's neck. With a knife, shape one end to fit the angle of the cone top.

14 Score and attach the neck, and finish its upper edge with a wooden tool.

15 If you wish, attach a lug or a handle.

VARIATION

Another all-extruded ewer can be made using hollow tube dies for the neck and spout, but not for the body. In this variation, the body is constructed from an extruded band (fig. 9 p. 69) circled and joined to create a cylinder.

Extruded and joined bands form the bodies and slab built cones form the tops of this ewer series.

After the cones have been stiffened upside down on their bodies (see above), they are inverted, joined to the bodies, and trimmed.

Ewers made using both solid and hollow dies

Extruded necks are fitted to the bodies and joined.

An extruded spout is carefully fitted to the shoulder of the ewer.

Ewers made using a combination of methods

COMBINATION METHODS

Spouted forms can be made using wheel-thrown as well as extruded parts. An advantage to mixing methods is that thrown bodies can be more round than extruded bodies, while extrusion easily creates necks, feet, spouts, and handles.

A variety of spouts thrown for a servies of ewers

Wheel thrown and trimmed cups and small dish forms can be scored and joined to form ewer bodies.

Extruded tubes or bands can be used for the necks and feet of ewers.

SQUARE HOLLOW DIES

Square hollow dies can be used to make some of the same things you can make with round ones—cups, teapots, vases, canisters, and a variety of sculptural works. They also allow you to easily create hard-edged forms, such as boxes. Boxes are an obvious item to make from hollow

square tubes, since the square hollow extrusion already has four sides. All that remains is to put on a top and bottom, and open the box in such a way that you create a lid. This section provides some general information about making boxes, along with a project to take you through creating your own.

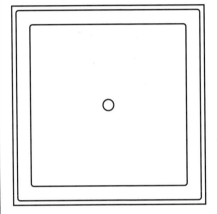

This die pattern is for use with a 5-inch square-barreled extruder with an internal die holder.

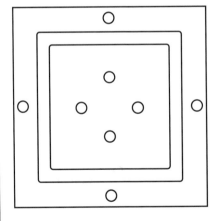

This die is also for use with a 5-inch square-barreled extruder; but this die is made with U-bolts, is self-supporting, and doesn't require an internal die holder.

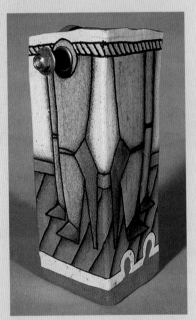

Top: D. HAYNE BAYLESS, *Sake Set.* Jar 6½ x 6 x 4 inches (16.25 x 15 x 10 cm, each cup 2.5 x 2 x 2 inches (6.25 x 5 x 5 cm). Stoneware; extruded; cone 10 reduction. Photo by artist.
Bottom: RIMAS VISGIRDA, *Vase*, 1992. 8 x 20 inches (20 x 50 cm); Stoneware with white englobe; extruded and altered; cone 10, 05, 018.

BOXES

The size and type of box you create is determined by the dimensions of your extruder and the uses you can envision for box shapes. Boxes that are too tall and narrow can be unstable; likewise, a box that is too long and narrow probably won't be useful for many things. One of the nice things about boxes is that they readily lend themselves to letting you invent your own uses for them.

Used with a square hollow die, a 4-inch (10 cm) round-barreled extruder will produce a tube up to 2¼ inches (5.6 cm) square. A 5-inch (12.5 cm) square-barreled model made with U-bolts can extrude a 3¼-inch (8.1 cm) square tube; if the die is suspended from an internal central die holder, a square extruder this size can make a

DAVID HENDLEY, *Extruded Hexagonal Jars*, 1992. 6 inches (15 cm) high. Stoneware; extruded with brass hinges; wood-fired to cone 10. Photo by Randy Mallory.

A hollow square die with an indented wall variation makes an interesting box form.

The user will know which way the lid goes on if the box is cut open with one side different from the others.

Traudi Thornton, *Sentinel*, 1997. 14½ x 4 x 4¼ inches (37 x 10 x 11 cm). Stoneware; extruded and extracted with additions; cone 8. Photo by artist.

4-inch clay tube. After attaching a slab bottom and top to the square extrusion (butt-joined for simplicity's sake), you can use the closed tube in either its vertical or horizontal orientation.

You can easily create a lid for a smaller box by cutting it open with a potter's knife or a modified cheese wire (with the roller removed). The best cheese wire to use for this purpose is one with the greatest distance between the wire and the slingshot-type handle, because it won't limit the depth of the lid as much as will a narrower version. You can also make your own wire harp by removing a hacksaw's blade and installing a wire in its place. The cheese wire is good for smaller items, the harp for larger.

Consider the lid before you cut the box open. For a small box, you can create a lid that doesn't need an internal flange to keep it in place by moving the wire a little up and down and diagonally as you cut open the box. The lid will have a positive fit even without an internal flange.

If you would rather cut a straight lid, use a sharp knife and a ruler. Cutting one side with a distinctive notch or shape will make it easy for the user to know which way to put the lid on. You can stabilize the lid by adding small pieces of clay that protrude slightly from the interior corners of the box. While it is possible to add a complete interior flange to give the lid a positive fit (and this is necessary for larger boxes), it's difficult and time consuming to do so for tiny boxes. Extruded feet and handles can also be added to simple box forms. Furniture such as wooden blanket boxes, old-fashioned hope chests and cedar chests can provide inspiration for additions to extruded boxes.

The same hollow extrsuion can be reoriented and cut open lengthwise to create a more "trunk"-like box

Larger extruders offer more possibilities for square box design. Box dies can be made with bellying curves on their sides and even attached ridges for feet, which can be wired away to leave furniture feet on the box corners. The lid can also be bellied or shaped for greater stability. Bellied and footed box forms are designed to be used in only one orientation, but the interesting shapes created compensate for the loss of flexibility.

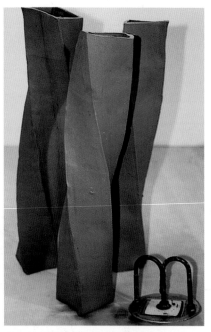

David Hendly likes to twist the square extrusions that he uses to make soap bottles.

Decorative extruded segments are added for feet.

A neck is added.

Another variation on box-making is to twist the forms soon after they come from the extruder and use these forms in an upright orientation. After adding slab bottoms and tops, the lid can be wired open. The twist moves the form away from the rigidity of extrusion, adding a nice liveliness to the box while still using a standard die shape.

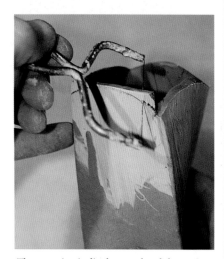

The extrusion is slip decorated and the top is trimmed with a cheese wire.

Top: DAVID HENDLEY, *Extruded Lotion Pots*, 1998. 8 inches (20 cm) high. Stoneware; extruded; wood-fired to cone 10.
Bottom: DAVID HENDLEY, *Frog Vase*, 1998. 5½ inches 13.75 cm) high. Stoneware; extruded and thrown with press-molded feet; wood-fired to cone 10. Photos by artist.

AN EXTRUDED BOX

TO MAKE A BOX LIKE THE ONE PICTURED, YOU WILL NEED:

20 POUNDS (9.08 KG) OF CLAY

EXTRUDER

A HOLLOW DIE, SQUARE OR VARIATION OF SQUARE

SHARP POTTER'S KNIFE

BRUSH AND WATER

SURFORM TOOL

SERRATED RIB

WOODEN TOOL

1 Begin by extruding two lengths of hollow square or shaped tube about 8 or 9 inches (20 or 22.5 cm) high.

2 Trim the bottom and top of one tube to make it level.

3 Cut open the other tube to create two wide panels (one each for the bottom and top of the box); this will leave two narrower panels. Save one of the narrow panels; discard the other.

4 Trim the length of one wide panel to fit the top of the tube. The shaped panel shown requires that notches be cut into the front and back of the tube body to make the top fit. Next, notches must be cut from the top on the remaining sides to make it conform to the body shape.

5 Score, dampen, and join the edges of the top and tube, then remove excess clay with a Surform plane and smooth the join with a sharp knife.

6 Turn the tube upside down and repeat steps 4 and 5 to make the bottom of the box.

7 Cut the box open to form a lid. Cut four narrow sections for a flange. Next, bevel cut the ends of flange sections to fit them into the lid corners. (You can put flanges on the box instead of the lid, if you prefer.)

8 Run the blunt end of a wooden tool around the inside seams of the box and around the flange seams to seal them.

9 Slip, glaze, and decorate the box according to your preferences.

VASES

The square tube also lends itself to vase-making, with stability an important consideration when determining the height of a vase made from a square tube. Easy variations in form can be made by canting the bottom of a hollow square extrusion to create a vase that leans a little, by cutting the top edge in a variety of ways, by cutting and curling bottom or top edges, and by joining multiple extrusions. Endless variations on vases from square clay tubes can be made by twisting, piercing, pinching, and joining or adding rims, textured extruded bands, and solid or hollow beads.

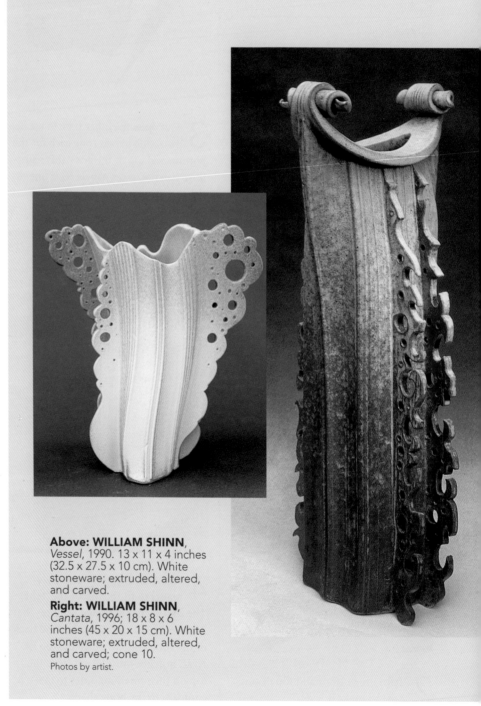

Above: WILLIAM SHINN, *Vessel*, 1990. 13 x 11 x 4 inches (32.5 x 27.5 x 10 cm). White stoneware; extruded, altered, and carved.

Right: WILLIAM SHINN, *Cantata*, 1996; 18 x 8 x 6 inches (45 x 20 x 15 cm). White stoneware; extruded, altered, and carved; cone 10.
Photos by artist.

CHAPTER TEN

TILES

PEWABIC POTTERY, *Fireplace*, 1985.
Stoneware; foot-pressed field tile and
extruded trim; cone 10 reduction.

THE MANUAL EXTRUDER is an excellent tool for making tiles. It makes lengths of flat or shaped clay ribbons that can be cut to size either when raw or after biscuit firing. You can use an extruder to make field and bullnose tiles, and moldings—finished shapes, or pieces to be further processed by mold or ram pressing. Extruded tiles can be smooth or textured, large or small, thick or thin, hard- or cushion-edged, with grooves or a smooth surface on the back. By curving and cutting extruded tiles, or cutting and joining them when they are still raw, you can create tiles in special or unusual shapes.

DIE DESIGN FOR EXTRUDED TILES

PLAIN

If you are working with a 4-inch (10 cm) extruder, you'll find that a plain tile die, about ⅜ inch (9 mm) thick x 3¼ inches (8.1 cm) wide with a grooved back (see fig. 1) is a useful size to include in your die repertoire.

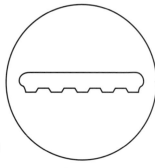

Figure 1

A reasonable length of tile to extrude in one pull is about 2 feet; placing tile extrusions on wooden boards as soon as they come out of the extruder makes it easier to move them around.

TEXTURED

While the back surfaces of tiles must be smooth (or grooved) and flat to facilitate installation, the top surfaces can be textured in a variety of ways. Dies can be drilled and filed to incorporate

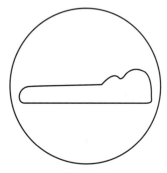

Figure 2

Top: DIANA PANCIOLI FOR PEWABIC POTTERY, *Detroit People Mover Cadillac Station (detail),* 1986. Stoneware; extruded and press molded; reduction fired to cone 10. Photo by artist.

Bottom: Paul Lewing, *Mt. Rainier/Fields Trivet,* 1998. 15 x 9 x 1 inches (37.5 x 22.5 x 2.5 cm). Porcelain; tile with extruded border; cone 5. Photo by Roger Schreiber.

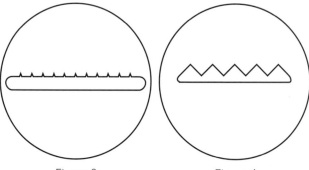

Figure 3   Figure 4

beads, corrugations, crenellations, or striations on the surface—any texture you invent that can be cut, filed, or drilled into the die. Figures 2, 3, and 4 show examples of some dies for textured tiles.

In the past, the backs of tiles were corrugated to make sure they stuck to the wall. Corrugation increased the tile's surface area and insured a good "mud" (cement) set. Today, setting cements include bond-insuring epoxy additives, so the backs of tiles need not be corrugated. Tiles that are corrugated, however, may be lighter and dry flatter.

With a sharp knife, a plastic square, and marks made at the edge of the table, extrusions are easily cut into tiles.

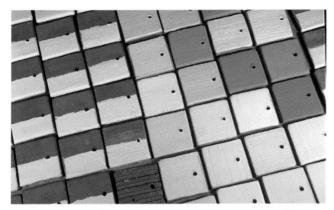

These test tiles, designed for display in the studio, were extruded, cut, slip painted, and drilled for hanging.

TEST TILES

Extrusion makes great glaze test tiles—a T-shaped die works well for standing tiles, and a plain die for flat tiles. Holes pierced in either shape will allow for stringing or for nailing up in the studio. Figure 5 shows a T-shaped die for test tiles.

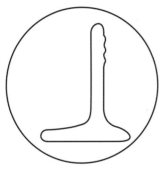

Figure 5

MAKING AND USING EXTRUDED TILES

You can comfortably extrude a 2-foot length of tile in one pull; tile extrusions placed on wood boards as soon as they are out of the extruder will be easier to move around. Kinks in a tile extrusion can be straightened by pressing the extrusion against the straight edge of a piece of wood. Or, if you place the extrusion at the edge of a table, you can straighten it by gently pressing its edges with a board. You can mark ruler lines (as a cutting guide) either on the board the extrusion is on or on the table edge, and use a plastic

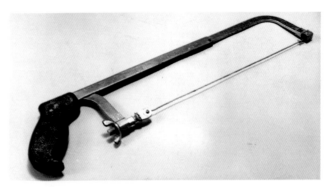

A harp is a hacksaw strung with a wire instead of a blade. It is useful for cutting tiles.

square and sharp knife to cut the tiles to size. A wooden miter box can also be used to cut the tiles; you can place the extrusions on boards (1 x 3 x 24 inches [2.5 x 7.5 x 60 cm] or 1 x 4 x 24 inches [2.5 x 10 x 60 cm]) that fit through the center of a miter box, and cut the tiles to size with a wire harp. (A "harp" is a hacksaw strung with a taught wire instead of a blade.)

The length of a border tile is cut to equal two smaller tiles plus one grout joint.

If you're planning to use different lengths of tiles in an installation, it's a good idea to cut the different lengths so that they create a unified "system." For example, if one square tile is the width of the die (3¼ inches [8.1 cm]), cut a few tiles and place them on the table arranged with the desired space for grout between them. Then cut a longer tile which will equal the length of two square tiles plus one grout joint (or, for a longer tile, three tiles plus two grout joints). You can also integrate the lengths of molding pieces, decorative strips, and bullnose tiles into the system in this way.

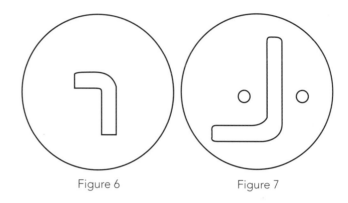

Figure 6   Figure 7

the inside wall of a miter box; the miter box wall will keep the extrusion straight while cutting. Figures 6 and 7 show different dies for bullnose tiles.

About 2 feet of molding, bullnose, or tile extrusion can be made in one pull.

Pewabic Pottery counter detail; extruded trim showing miter cut and joined corner

Although making perfect tiles might be possible, it is not always desirable. The crudest tiles, when set, can be the most beautiful. The great thing about hand-made tiles is that they *look* handmade—a few kinks here or there can lend charm to the whole. (In fact, one commercial tile manufacturer purposely leaves deep finger marks on the edges of ram-pressed tiles to give them a handmade look.) Some of the imperfections the extrusion process produces are handsome and interesting, so try to examine them with fresh eyes. If you find yourself looking for perfection, you may be using the industrial model you are accustomed to as a measure—better to be attentive to the process, and make judgements as they arise.

Extruded bullnose, or three-dimensional tiles, are a little more difficult to make than extruded flat tiles, because they need to be supported while they stiffen. This can be easily achieved, by draping them over the edge of a board (or two, depending on their thickness). When the bullnose is stiff and ready to be cut, place it on a board with the protrusion upward against

While in their uncut, freshly extruded state, tile lengths are easy to texture and color. You can apply slip colors, comb or press in textural accents, and then cut them into tiles. The disjointedness of the cut pattern when reassembled will add interest to the work, like the discontinuous patterns of Japanese Oribe ware. Pattern direction can also be manipulated. If the pattern is created in a direction parallel to the length of the extrusion, the cut segments can later be reoriented to advantage, adding variety and interest to the original lengthwise orientation.

Tiles can be dried on or between sheets of drywall. Metal racks, which allow air all around the tiles while they are drying, help prevent warping. Tiles can be dried on wooden boards under plastic until their top surfaces are firm (overnight), and then turned upside down on a fresh dry board to continue drying under plastic. Slow drying will cause less warpage than fast drying. When drying tiles, it is best to lay them face down. It is best if tiles dry flat, but if they don't, it is better if their corners curl slightly downward (the tiles hump slightly in the center). For this reason, drying tiles on their faces is preferable to drying them on their backs; if they warp (curl upward) while drying upside down, they warp in a favorable direction.

Warped tiles—especially those that warp upwards at the corners—are very hard to grout, and don't make for good installation. If differences in thickness cause your tiles to warp, you may need to alter the design of your tile. Longer, narrower, or pointed shapes such as triangles are more difficult to dry without warping. If your tiles warp badly, they might be too thin for the shape you have made, and thickening them will make them dry flatter. The trick is to check on your tiles daily to see how they are drying. They can be turned, stacked, or weighted to help keep them flat.

Left: SHEL NEYMARK, Detail, *Rosalie Doolittle Fountain*, 1996. 60 feet (1800 cm) of extrusions, each 5 x 1 inches (12.5 x 2.5 cm). Low-absorption clay body; extruded and formed on site; cone 02. Photo by Herb Lotz.

Above right: SHEL NEYMARK, *Balcony Handrail*, 1998. Handrail 20 feet (600 cm) long, each extrusion 12 x 6 x 3 inches (30 x 15 x 7.5 cm). Low-absorption clay body; extruded; cone 02. Photo by artist.

Below right: SHEL NEYMARK, *Stair Handrail*, 1996. 32 x 4 x 6 inches (80 x 10 x 15 cm). Raku; extruded; cone 04. Photo by Robert Reck.

PROJECT
A TILED COUNTERTOP

50 LBS. (22.7 KG) OF CLAY BODY

1 CUP OF SLIP

2 OR 3 DIES: 1 TILE DIE (FIG. 1) AND 1
BULLNOSE DIE (FIG. 6); AND
1 DECORATIVE STRIP/BAND (OPTIONAL)

A PLASTIC SHEET

EXTRUDER

3 OR 4 WOOD BOARDS
1 x 3 x 24 INCHES AND
1 x 4 x 24 INCHES (1 OR 2 OF EACH)

3 PLYWOOD 1 x 2'S (WARE BOARDS)

BRUSH (SMALL)

SLIP AND COMBING TOOLS
(OPTIONAL)

PLASTIC BAT

RULER

PENCIL OR MARKER

PLASTIC SQUARE

POTTER'S KNIFE (SHARP)

WIRE HARP (OPTIONAL)

MITER BOX (OPTIONAL)

1 Using your tile die, extrude about 20 lbs. (9.08 kg) of clay in 2-foot (60 cm) lengths. (After cutting, this will yield about 3 square feet [.27m²] of tile.) Place the extrusions face up on ware boards and straighten them by pressing against the edge of one long side of each extrusion with a wooden board.

2 Next, use your bullnose die to extrude about 10 lbs. (4.54 kg) of clay. (After cutting, this will yield about 8 feet [240 cm] of tile.) Place the extrusions on long boards with the shallow edge of the bullnose hanging over the edge of the board. Gently straighten the extrusions by pressing a board against one edge, then set them aside to stiffen a little.

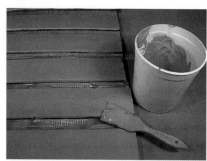

3 Brush the tile extrusions you created in step 1 with slip, texture them if you wish, or leave them plain.

If you choose to comb textures onto the tile surface, an inexpensive plastic tool from the hardware store for spreading adhesive can be cut into varying widths to use as combing tools.

4 Before you try out your combing technique on the actual tile extrusion, you can practice by putting wet slip on a plastic bat. Comb through the slip, using a brush to erase marks or patterns you don't want, until you find a pattern you like. Set the extrusions aside for an hour to allow the slip and tile to stiffen a little before cutting the extrusions into tile lengths.

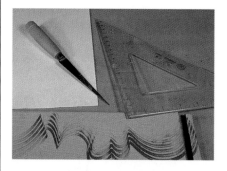

5 The next step is to use a ruler and pencil or marker to measure and mark the edge of your worktable in preparation for cutting your tiles. For square tile like those shown, first measure the width of your extrusion—this measurement

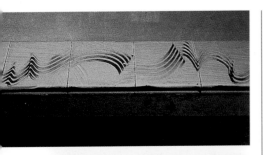

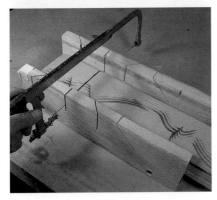

indicates how far apart your marks should be spaced. Here, the marks are 3⅛ inches (7.8 cm) apart, since the extrusion's width is 3⅛ inches (7.8 cm). Place the extrusion at the edge of the table and straighten it once more with a wood board. Using a plastic square as a guide, cut tiles with a sharp knife (or use a miter box and harp). If your plastic square sticks to the tile face, wait a little longer for the slip to dry, or use a clean piece of paper between the tile and the square to prevent sticking.

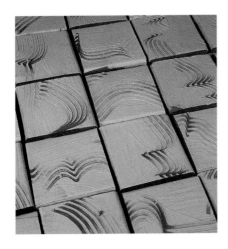

6   After cutting, place the tiles face up on a wooden board.

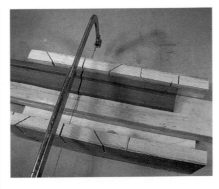

7   Cut the bullnose extrusion to lengths you prefer for your countertop—twice the length of the tiles (plus the length of one grout joint) will work well.

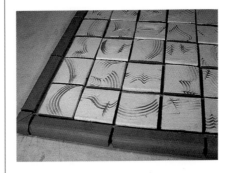

8   At this point, you can lay out your countertop, placing plain tiles with space for a grout joint between them and fitting bullnose tiles around the perimeter of the grouped tiles. Create any corners you need by miter-cutting two pieces of bullnose tile, then scoring to join them. Allow the tiles to stiffen overnight under a sheet of lightweight plastic.

9   Using your knife or Surform tool, refine the tiles by rounding the cut edges on each plain tile, and on both ends of each bullnose tile.

There are two reasons for doing this—glaze pulls away from sharp edges, and sharp edges chip. Rounding the cut edges of the tiles removes some of the slip, so if you have slipped your tiles, you might want to re-slip those edges and, if you choose, the bullnose tiles, too.

10   Lay out your countertop on a ware board or on your work surface, and critique your design at this point. It is still possible to alter the design—one of the benefits of tile is its flexibility. Dry your tiles upside down under plastic for a few days, then uncovered until they are dry enough to biscuit fire.

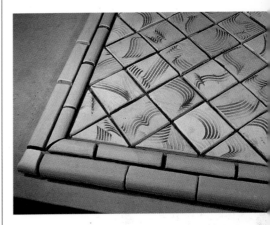

11   (Optional) If you prefer visual interest at your tile countertop's, you can cut some of the square tiles in half to create triangular tiles, and alter your countertop pattern. You can also extrude and add a decorative strip between the bullnose and field tiles. The pattern shown, laid on the diagonal and using triangles at the edges, requires that the bullnose tiles be cut shorter to match the triangles' lengths. Glaze, of course, will add a whole new dimension to the design.

12   Install and grout the countertop in your desired location.

MOLDED TILES

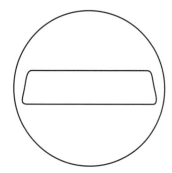

Figure 8

Extrusion can be helpful when making press-molded tiles. An extrusion as wide as your tile mold opening and twice as thick as the mold's depth, when cut into tile-sized lengths, will

Plaster molds for embossed 3 x 3 inch tiles are filled with extruded clay segments.

The extruded clay is first thumb pressed into the mold, then pounded with a rubber mallet.

Excess clay is removed from the tile backs with a wire harp.

Two press molded, embossed 3 x 3 inch tiles.

fill the mold with the correct amount of clay for efficient pressing. After the clay is pressed and pounded into the mold with a cloth-covered rubber mallet, excess clay can be wire-cut off the back of the tile with a harp. Figure 8 shows a die for the above-described use with press-molded tiles.

POWER EXTRUDED TILES

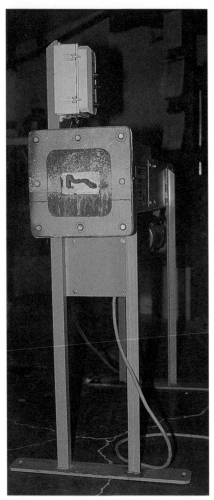

Pictured above is the extruding end of the RR-V8 tile maker from Radical Ridge showing a bullnose die in place, ready to extrude.

Power extrusion offers the capability of producing tiles in sufficient quantity to operate a production tile business, but it also generates problems not encountered in the manual extrusion process. With hand-powered extrusion, the speed of extrusion is controllable; with powered extrusion, it has not been until some recent changes by one manufacturer. In general, problems with extrusion are amplified when augor and/or power drive become part of the process. Clay flow problems are more serious and subtle, and the moisture content of clays becomes more significant. For use in power extrusion, dies must be sturdier, more carefully designed, and smoother, and baffles must be used to combat clay flow problems. Power extruder users recommend either plywood or UHMW plastic for die materials. UHMW is harder to work with and difficult to sand, but provides fine detail and wears well. Wide, thin extrusions are the most difficult to make.

Nevertheless, there are machines designed to extrude tile in large quantity, and people who operate successful businesses using them. In addition to an extruding pugmill system with a special tile nozzle, Bluebird Manufacturing supplies extruding tables (to reduce necessary handling of fresh extrusions), cutting systems, and an internal die holder.

Another tile machine available, the RR-V8 from Radical Ridge Pottery, is a non-hydraulic, electrically operated plunger-style extruder. It eliminates augur memory problems and pulsing associated with studio pugmills, and its variable speed helps compensate for changes in clay consistency.

These three beautiful fireplaces show the fine handmade tiles made by North Prairie Tileworks, a company based in Minnesota.

CHAPTER ELEVEN

A GALLERY OF SCULPTURE

Above left: INGE PEDERSON, *Blue Tradition*, 1998. 72 x 68 x 8 inches (180 x 170 x 20 cm). Stoneware; 300 extruded modules, each 5½ inches (13 x 13 cm).

Above right: INGE PEDERSON, Detail, *Blue Tradition*. Photos by Terje Agnalt.

SOME ARTISTS BEGIN with an idea, using any medium to create the sculptural work they have in mind; others work toward an idea using a chosen material as their starting point. Potters often do the latter—fall in love with clay, and use it as the starting point for exploration. With extrusion, you can use both the tool and the material to pursue an idea, or allow the extruder and the forms it produces guide your exploration.

The pleasure of working with extruded "parts" is similar to the childhood pleasure of playing with construction toys…blocks, Legos, Tinkertoys. Extruded forms—made in multiples, in infinite variety, and as hollow volumes—provide a challenge to the artist which is similar to working with found objects. Extrusion can provide shapes you hadn't planned on that inspire solutions you never imagined. Whether you choose to make sculpture that is small or large, abstract or figurative, wall-hung or freestanding, extrusion offers numerous possibilities.

MELISSA GASKINS, *Secret Garden*, 1990-91. 14 x 10 x 12 inches (35 x 25 x 30 cm). White earthenware; extruded and assembled; cone 06 and 019.

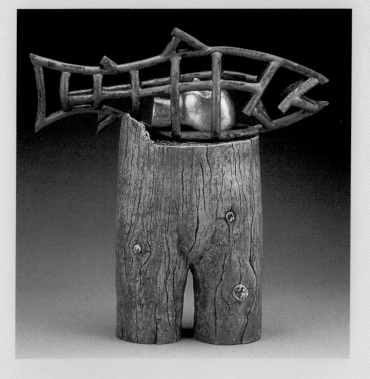

Top: TED VOGEL, *Cup Cage*, 1997. 18 x 15 inches (45 x 37.5 cm). Earthenware with terra sigilattas and gold leaf; extruded and other.
Bottom: TED VOGEL, *Fish Cage*, 1997. 23 x 22 inches (57.5 x 55 cm). Earthenware with terra sigilattas and gold leaf; extruded and other.

"*While I am primarily a wheel-throwing potter, I have been using the extruder regularly since 1982. ...I am not interested in repeating [extruded] forms. I want to keep my extruded forms as opposites, as a balance to the repeated forms of the wheel.*"

MALCOLM WRIGHT

Top: SERGIO DE GIUSTI, *Visceral Expressionism*, 1974. 20 x 30 inches (50 x 75 cm). Stoneware; extruded and altered; cone 04.

Bottom right: MALCOLM WRIGHT, *Rocking Vase*, 1996. 6 x 9 x 8 inches (15 x 22.5 x 20 cm). Stoneware; extruded and altered; cone 13. left-hand column photo

Bottom left: MALCOLM WRIGHT, *Angle Vase*, 1995. 5½ x 11½ x 9 inches (13.75 x 28.75 x 22.5 cm). Stoneware; extruded and altered; cone 10.

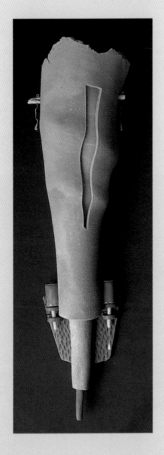

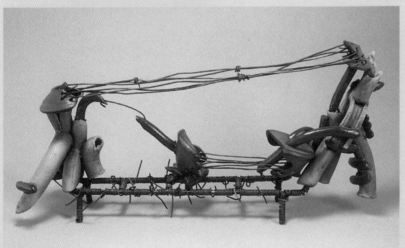

Clockwise from top left: KATHY TRIPLETT, *Wall Sconce*, 1998. 26 x 10 x 5 inches (65 x 25 x 12.5 cm). Earthenware; extruded, handbuilt, slab; cone 05.

VIRGINIA SCOTCHIE, *Linear Formations*, 1994. 20 x 12 x 14 inches (50 x 30 x 35 cm) each. Red earthenware; extruded, altered, and assembled; cone 04.

TRAUDI THORNTON, *Casablanca*, 1997. 11¾ x 4¾ x 5½ inches (30 x 12 x 14 cm). Stoneware; extruded and assembled; cone 8.

LEON POPIK, *Caught In Between*, 1996. 10½ x 27 x 7½ inches (26.25 x 67.5 x 18.75 cm), Stoneware; extruded, wheel-thrown, assembled; cone o6, 9.

All photos by artists.

FIGURATIVE WORKS

Extruded tubes of all sizes have been used as the figurative structural elements to depict the human body (torso and limbs, and more) in ways both serious and whimsical.

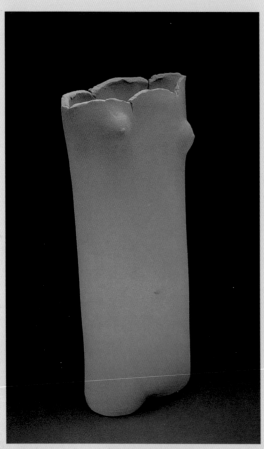

Clockwise from top left:
NILS LOU, *Torso Vessel*, 1988. 9 x 6-1/2 x 22 inches (22.5 x 16.25 x 55 cm). Stoneware; extruded and altered; cone 10 reduction.

JERRY CAPLAN working on *Gothic Figure*, an extruded "pipe sculpture."

JERRY CAPLAN, *Metamorphic Group*, 1973. 60 x 72 x 18 inches (150 x 180 x 45 cm). Terra-cotta; extruded and altered.

INSTALLATIONS

Once formed, extruded segments can be drilled and the pieces threaded and hung from walls or ceilings, nailed to walls, piled or arranged on floors, tables, chairs, and in corners. Hollow forms can be threaded on sticks and ropes for installation. Extrusion can be incorporated into furniture design, primarily as supports for tables, and used outdoors as columns and totems.

A number of artists have explored the ability to create similar forms in great quantity, and have used the mass of objects for installations.

Left: KATHY ORNISH, *Structural Form #25 (Incendiary)*, 1997. 43 x 72 x 42 inches (107.5 x 180 x 105 cm). Stoneware, steel, stones, wood, paint. Stoneware extruded, altered, and painted; cone 6.
Right: KATHY ORNISH, *Structural Form # 18 (Window Diptych)*, 1995. Size variable depending on installation site. Stoneware, steel, and paint. Stoneware extruded, altered, and painted; cone 04. Photos by artist.

"*The extruder offers a mechanized 'look' that represents the mechanization and industrialization predominant in the West since the Industrial Revolution. ... By using soft clay and working with it in the plastic state, I can impart a sense of humanness and softness through minor distortions, thereby giving the work a duality of man and machine.*"

RIMAS VISGIRDA

Top, bottom and right: DIANA PANCIOLI, Experimental Works Using Hollow Extrusions, 1988.

WALL WORK

Clay artists have tackled the weight problem of large clay sculptures by using honeycombs created of multiple hollow extrusions to support a work. Hollow extrusion as substructure can add depth to wall-hung works without adding excess weight. By breaking through to the layers below, the artist can use extrusions to play a visual part in the overlay, or the structure can remain hidden and simply support the work.

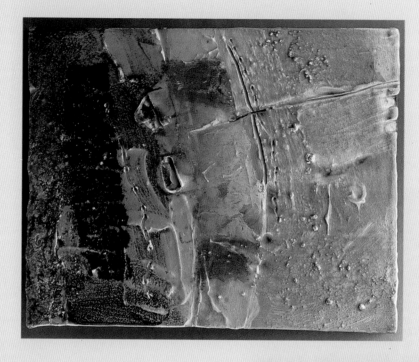

"As you can see, I prefer to allow the process to have a voice in itself. Why should it look like some other process formed it? I want to enjoy extrusions as extrusions and the unique feeling of pressure they evoke."

JOHN STEPHENSON

Top: JOHN H. STEPHENSON, *The Devil's Detail,* 1999. 22 x 17½ x 1⅛ inches (55 x 43.75 x 2.8 cm). White earthenware; extruded hollow tile, surface worked with thick slips; cone 02. Photo by artist.

Bottom: ESTHER HERNANDEZ, *Self Portrait,* 1998. 18 x 24 inches 45 x 60 cm). Terra-cotta; extruded understructure with applied slabs; cone 04. Photo by Diana Pancioli.

"When I use the extruder, in most cases I do not want the finished product to "look" extruded. ... A sign of success, for me, is when another potter sees something I've made using the extruder, and can't figure out how it was made."

DAVID HENDLEY

Top: SANDRA WESTLEY, *burden: wagon #4 from the sticks and stones series*, 1997. 17 x 24 x 23 inches (42.5 x 60 x 57.5 cm). Buff-colored sculpture body; extruded, slab-built, and assembled; cone 1, 05. Photo by artist.

Center: LISA MERIDA-PAYTES, *Flight of the Tribbles*, 1997. 13 to 36 inches (32.5 x 90 cm) high. Stoneware; extruded, handbuilt, and carved; cone 2 reduction. Photo by Jay Bachemin.

Bottom: ROY HANSCOM, *Untitled*, 1979. 42 x 42 x 42 inches ((105 x 105 x 105 cm). Stoneware; extruded and altered.

COMPOSITE WORKS

Sculpture can begin with extrusion, but be manipulated and combined with other processes to the point that its origins as extrusion are hardly evident in the final work. A philosophical argument arises around this point: Some sculptors feel that the extrusion process should be evident in an extruded work—that it should be used for what it is. Others believe that extrusion should be disguised and altered from its original state. However you choose to use extrusion, I think you will find it an engaging process that challenges and enhances your creative work with clay.

Clockwise from top left: MARK SCHOENLIEBER, *Two Tables and a Plant Stand*. Front table 20 inches (50 cm) high, back table 30 inches (75 cm) high, plant stand 30 inches (75 cm) high. Stoneware; extruded, wheel-thrown, and assembled; cone 5. Photo by artist.
BENNETT BEAN, *Slate Top Production Table*. 66 x 29 x 24 inches (165 x 72.5 x 60 cm). Red earthenware; extruded and press molded; cone 06. Photo by artist.
LINDA DOHERTY, *Bird Cage*, 1997. 32 x 22 x 22 inches (80 x 55 x 55 cm). Sculpture clay; extruded, thrown, pressed, and assembled; cone 04, 06. Photo by Ken Mayer of KM Studios.

Clockwise from top: ROBERT HARRISON, *Cullumned Spiral*, 1989. 9 x 25 feet (270 x 750 cm). Glazed porcelain shards, concrete, marble slabs. Kohler Sculpture Park, Kohler, Wisconsin.

BENNETT BEAN, *Pergola*. 10 x 12 x 12 feet (25 x 30 x 30 cm). Red earthenware; extruded and press molded; cone 06.

FRANCISCO JIMINEZ, *Obelisk*, 1996. 84 x 17 x 13 inches (210 x 42.5 x 32.5 cm). Terra-cotta; extruded (through an industrial press), carved, and sculpted; cone 2. Photo by artist.

"*What fascinates me so much about the extrusion process is what can be accomplished after the extrusion has come from the die. The invitation to alter the form is implicit. The question is: How much, and when to do so?! Cutting, gusseting, imprinting, or handbuilding onto extrusions are just a few of the good options. Did I say the extrusion exits the die? So much can be done as the shapes leave the die mouth as well! Moving the flowing clay form rhythmically (or not) against the edge of the die as it exits can produce interesting marks or alter the form itself, overcoming the inclination of extruded forms to appear…well, at times, too extruded.*"

JOHN GLICK

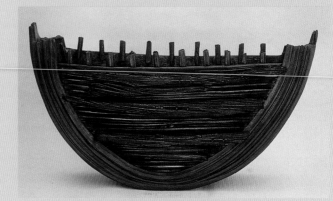

Clockwise from top left:
JOHN GLICK, *Wall Relief "Mantel Series,"* 1997. 18 x 7½ x 6 inches (45 x 18.75 x 15 cm). Stoneware; extruded, altered, and wheel-thrown, with press molded additions; cone 10. Photo by artist.

LAURIE ROLLAND, *Ship of Isis*, 1997. 11¼ x 16 x 5 inches (28 x 40 x 13 cm). Stoneware; extruded, slab-built, and assembled; cone 6. Photo by artist.

LAURIE ROLLAND, *Badarian Vessel*, 1997. 4¾ x 11½ x 7½ inches (12 x 29 x 19 cm). Stoneware; extruded, slab-built, wheel-thrown, and assembled; cone 6. Photo by artist.

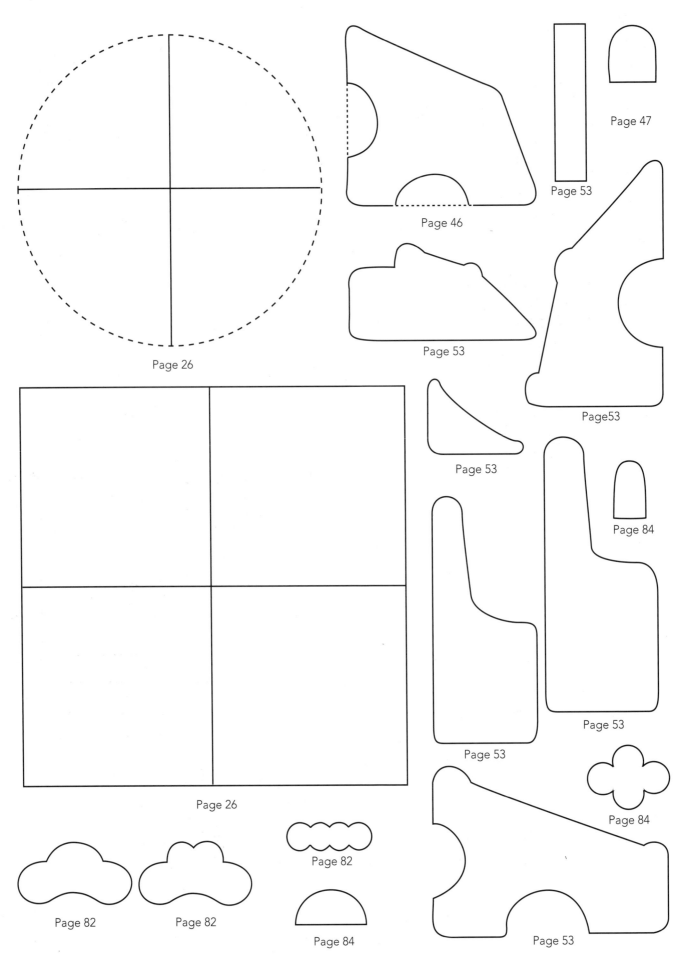

Page 26

Page 46

Page 53

Page 47

Page 53

Page 53

Page 53

Page 84

Page 26

Page 53

Page 53

Page 84

Page 82

Page 82

Page 82

Page 82

Page 84

Page 53

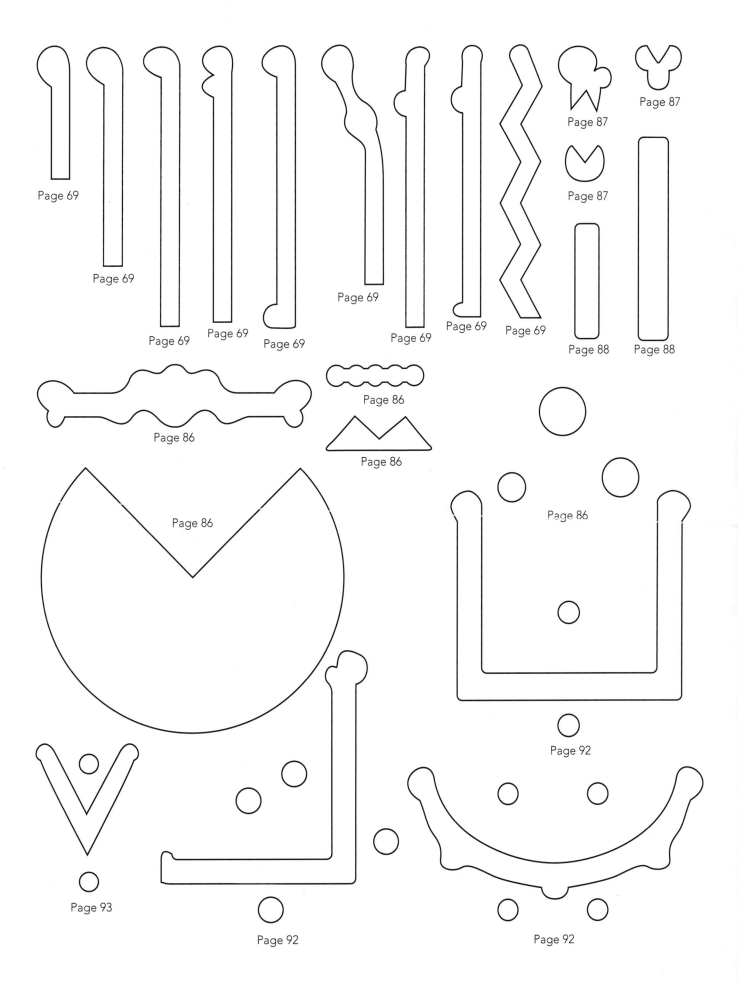

Page 69

Page 69

Page 69

Page 69

Page 69

Page 69

Page 69

Page 69

Page 87

Page 87

Page 87

Page 88

Page 88

Page 86

Page 86

Page 86

Page 86

Page 86

Page 92

Page 93

Page 92

Page 92

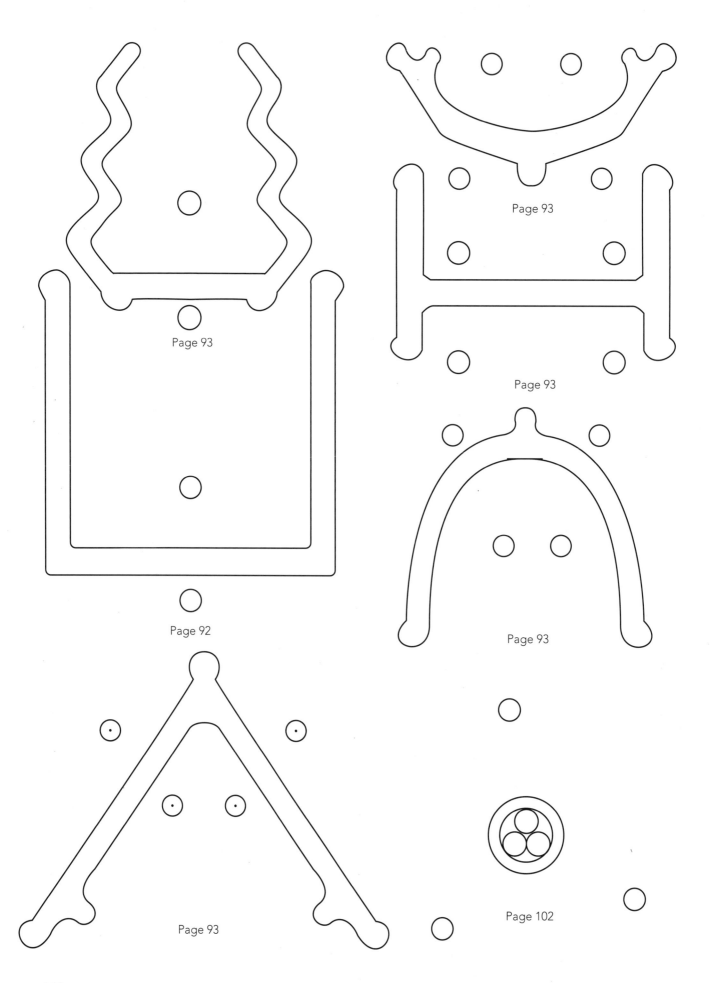

Page 93

Page 93

Page 93

Page 92

Page 93

Page 93

Page 102

140

Page 118

Page 118

Page 118

Page 118

Page 112

Page 119

Page 112

Page 120

Page 124

Page 120

141

ACKNOWLEDGEMENTS

I would like to thank Eastern Michigan University for the Spring/Summer Research Grant, which provided me with the time and funding to begin this book, and Lark Books for helping me finish it. Special thanks to Dr. Robert Holkeboer of E.M.U's Graduate Division, for advice, cameras, and travel support; also to my colleagues Roy Johnston and Tom Venner, for their encouragement and assistance. My gratitude also to Steven Branfman of The Potter's Shop, David Gamble of Amaco, and Kathy Dambach, for their letters of support.

Thanks, too, to E.M.U. graduate students Beth Ogden and Catherine Shinnick, who assisted me with the book's how-to photographs, and to my undergraduate students for their interest and support; to Ron Ruth of Rovin Ceramics for giving advice on a moment's notice; to Dremel Tool for providing the right bits; and to all the manufacturers—Bluebird, Bailey, North Star, Randall, Super Duper, Radicalridge, and North Prairie Tileworks—and artists, who answered my questions. Heartfelt thanks to the many artists who graciously submitted images of their work for inclusion in the book, and to the Clayart Listserv for information and assistance. I would like to express my thanks, too, to Art Director Kathy Holmes, for her patience and skillful book design.

My daughter, sister, family, friends, and editor, Danielle Truscott, deserve medals for putting up with the ravings of a first-time author. And a medal to Frank Jones for his encouragement and understanding.

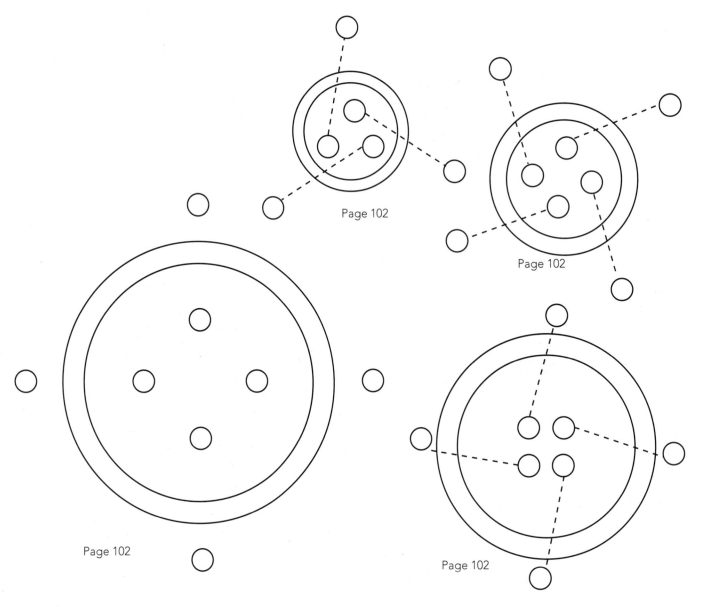

Page 102

Page 102

Page 102

Page 102

BIBLIOGRAPHY

CONTRIBUTING ARTISTS

Birks, Tony. *The Complete Potter's Companion.* Boston, Toronto, London: Little, Brown, Bulfinch Books, 1996.

Casson, Michael. *The Craft of the Potter.* Hauppauge: Barron's Educational Series, 1979.

Chavarria, Joaquim. *The Big Book of Ceramics.* New York: Watson-Guptill, 1994.

Clayton, Pierce. *The Clay Lover's Guide to Making Molds.* Asheville, NC: Lark Books, 1998.

Cooper, Emmanuel. *The Complete Potter: Glazes.* London: Batsford, 1992.

Cosentino, Peter. *The Encyclopedia of Pottery Techniques.* Philadelphia: Running Press, 1990.

Davis, Don. *Wheel-Thrown Ceramics.* Asheville, NC: Lark Books, 1998.

Giorgini, Frank. *Handmade Tiles.* Asheville, NC: Lark Books, 1994

Gregory, Ian. *Sculptural Ceramics.* London: A&C Black, 1992.

Hamer, Frank, and Hamer, Janet. *The Potter's Dictionary of Materials and Techniques.* Philadelphia: University of Pennsylvania, 1991.

King, Peter. *Architectural Ceramics for the Studio Potter.* Asheville, NC: Lark Books, 1999.

Levy, Mike. *Decorated Earthenware.* London: Batsford, 1992.

Nigrosh, Leon. *Sculpting Clay.* Worcester, Mass: Davis, 1992.

Peters, Lynn. *Surface Decoration for Low-Fire Ceramics.* Asheville, NC: Lark Books, 1999.

Peterson, Susan. *The Craft and Art of Clay.* Englewood Cliffs, NY: Prentice-Hall, 1996.

Rhodes, Daniel. *Clay and Glazes for the Potter.* Radnor, PA: Chilton, 1973.

Rhodes, Daniel. *Stoneware and Porcelain: The Art of High-Fired Pottery.* Radnor, PA: Chilton Book Company, 1959.

Rossol, Monona. *The Artist's Complete Health and Safety Guide.* New York: Allworth Press, 1990.

Speight, Charlotte F., and Toki, John. *Hands in Clay: An Introduction to Ceramics.* 3rd ed. Mountain View, CA: Mayfield, 1995.

The Ceramic Design Book: A Gallery of Contemporary Work. Asheville, NC: Lark Books, 1998.

Triplett, Kathy. *Handbuilt Ceramics.* Asheville, NC: Lark Books, 1997.

Waller, Jane. *Hand-Built Ceramics.* London: Batsford, 1996.

Woody, Elsbeth S. *Handbuilding Ceramic Forms.* New York: Farrar Straus Giroux, 1978.

D. Hayne Bayless (pages 94, 112), Ivoryton, Connecticut

Bennett Bean (pages 135, 136), Blairstown, New Jersey

Marla Bollak (page 64), Black Mountain, North Carolina

Frank Bosco (pages 13, 41, 43, 67, 94, 100, 105), Millburn, New Jersey

Elina Brandt-Hansen (pages 51, 85), Klokkarvik, Norway

Richard Burkett (page 103), San Diego, California

Jerry Caplan (page 130), Pittsburgh, Pennsylvania

Stephanie Cionca (page 84), Plymouth, Michigan

Ginny Conrow (page 105) Seattle, Washington

Kathy Dambach (pages 9, 35), Farmington Hills, Michigan

Harris Deller (pages 103, 105), Carbondale, Illinois

Linda Doherty (page 135), Burnaby, British Columbia, Canada

Melissa Gaskins (page 127), East Norriton, Pennsylvania

Sergio De Giusti (page 128), Redford Township, Michigan

John Glick (pages 8, 75, 91, 92, 105, 106, 137) Farmington Hills, Michigan

Roy Hanscom (page 134), Kingwood, Texas

Steve Hansen (page 25), Berrien Springs, Michigan

Robert Harrison (page 104, 136), Helena, Montana

David Hendley (pages 18, 27, 66, 112, 114, 134), Maydelle, Texas

Esther Hernandez (page 133), Ferndale, Michigan

Brian Hively (page 71), West Columbia, South Carolina

Ayumi Hori (page 68), Seattle, Washington

Francisco Jiminez (page 136), Campbell, California

Randy Johnston (pages 6, 15, 64, 73, 79), River Falls, Wisconsin

Walter Keeler (pages 21, 102, 106), Penallt, Monmouth, United Kingdom

Mikel Kelley (page 79), Mt. Horeb, Wisconsin

Michael Kifer (page 112), Richland, Michigan

Bob Kinzie (page 83), Aptos, California

Phyllis Kudder-Sullivan (page 84), Shoreham, New York

Jennifer Lapham (page 42), Chicago, Illinois

Ty Larsen (page 63), Asheville, North Carolina

Young Lee (page 90), Seoul, Korea

Paul Lewing (pages 94, 118), Seattle, Washington

Nils Lou (pages 18, 105, 130), Willamina, Oregon

Diana Manchak (page 64), Accokeek, Maryland

Ginny Marsh (page 60), Borden, Illinois

Lisa Merida-Paytes (page 134), Cinti, Ohio

Shel Neymark (page 121), Embudo, New Mexico

Kathy Ornish (page 131), Lansing, Michigan

Shirl Parmentier (pages 82, 85), Fly Creek, New York

Inge Pedersen (pages 36, 126), Oslo, Norway

Rina Peleg (pages 57, 80, 81), Brooklyn, New York

Leon Popik (pages 77, 129), Calgery, Alberta, Canada

I. B. Remsen (pages 65, 92), Ann Arbor, Michigan

Jim Robison (pages 19, 100), Holmfirth, Huddersfield, England

Laurie Rolland (pages 57, 137) Sechelt, British Columbia, Canada

Mark Schoenleber (page 135), Ashland, Oregon

Virginia Scotchie (page 129), Columbia, South Carolina

Phillip Sellers (page 81) Madison, Ohio

Michael Sherrill (pages 16, 19), Hendersonville, North Carolina

William Shinn (pages 39, 116), Santa Maria, California

Lewis Snyder (page 19), Murfreesboro, Tennessee

Frank Stella (pages 67, 100), Millburn, New Jersey

John H. Stephenson (pages 22, 23, 133), Ann Arbor, Michigan

Susanne Stephenson (page 34), Ann Arbor, Michigan

Nancy Stoll (page 90), Ann Arbor, Michigan

Paul Stubbs (page 19, 65), Somerset, England

Traudi Thornton (pages 79, 113, 129), Wilmington, North Carolina

Kathy Triplett (page 129), Weaverville, North Carolina

John Troup (page 60), Bernville, Pennsylvania

Todd Turek (page 82), Juneau, Alaska

Tom Venner (page 67), Saline, Michigan

Rimas Visgirda (pages 101, 103, 132), Champagne, Illinois

Ted Vogel (page 127), Portland, Oregon

Sandra Westley (page 134), Ann Arbor, Michigan

Malcolm Wright (page 128), Marlboro, Vermont

INDEX